ALSO BY SALLY SAMPSON

The $50 Dinner Party

Recipes from the Night Kitchen:
A Practical Guide to Spectacular
Soups, Stews, and Chilies

BY SALLY SAMPSON AND TODD ENGLISH

The Figs Table

The Olives Table

BY SALLY SAMPSON AND LOIS L. LINDAUER

The Diet Workshop's Recipes for Healthy Living

THE
BakeSale
Cookbook

★ QUINTESSENTIAL AMERICAN DESSERTS ★

Sally Sampson

A FIRESIDE BOOK

Published by Simon & Schuster
New York • London • Toronto • Sydney • Singapore

FIRESIDE
Rockefeller Center
1230 Avenue of the Americas
New York, NY 10020

FIRESIDE and colophon are registered trademarks
of Simon & Schuster, Inc.
Designed by Jill Weber

Manufactured in the United States of America

1   3   5   7   9   10   8   6   4   2

Library of Congress Cataloging-in-Publication Data
Sampson, Sally
The bakesale cookbook : quintessential American desserts / Sally Sampson.
p. cm.
"A Fireside book."
Includes index.
1. Desserts. I. Title.
TX773.S29 2000
641.8'6–dc21   99-086270
ISBN 0-684-86229-8

ACKNOWLEDGMENTS

I cannot thank Paige Retus and Bercie Travers enough. It is true that I could have done this book without them, but I would've gained twice as many pounds and it would have taken an additional six months and, after all that, it wouldn't have been half as good. And, of course, I thank Sydny Miner, Carla Glasser, Jenny Alperen, Andrea Mullins, and Beth Wareham.

FOR MY TOTALLY ENCHANTING CHILDREN: **Ben**,
WHO OFFERS HIS "COMPLIMENTS TO THE CHEF" AT
ALMOST EVERY MEAL, AND **Lauren**, WHO, WHEN
SHE DISCOVERED THAT I HAD MADE THE BROWNIE SHE
WAS SAVORING (ENGAGEMENT BROWNIES, PAGE 82),
DECLARED ITS TASTE "PROFESSIONAL."
THEY BOTH KNOW THEIR WAY
AROUND MY HEART AND MY KITCHEN.

FOR **Mark,** MY ALWAYS HUNGRY HUSBAND,
WHO JOYFULLY ATE HIS WAY THROUGH THIS BOOK.

Contents

BARS ★ 75

All-American Brownies ★ Upstairs at the Pudding's Bourbon Brownies ★ Double-Decker Chocolate and Coconut Brownies ★ Engagement Brownies ★ Cream Cheese Brownies ★ Peanut Butter Brownies ★ Gretchen Taylor's Three-Layer Mint Brownies ★ Rocky Road Bars ★ Shirley's Chocolate Pecan Bourbon Bars ★ Pecan Turtle Bars ★ Chocolate Coconut Bars ★ Butterscotch–White Chocolate Brownies ★ Aunt Suzy's Chocolate Chip Gooey Bars ★ Melanie's Grandma's Kansas Rhubarb Shortbread ★ Sesame Apricot Bars ★ Coconut Toffee Bars ★ Lemon-Glazed Pecan and Coconut Squares ★ Amy Bodiker's Lemon Bars ★ Eleanor Rashkind's Toffee Squares ★ Barbara Haber's Rugelach ★ Apple Kuchen ★ Crisp Rice Treats ★ The Late Jake and Earl's Seven-Layer Bars ★ Apple Cranberry Oatmeal Bars ★

BREAKFAST, POUND, AND TEA CAKES, CUPCAKES, AND BABY CAKES ★ 124

Buttery Pound Cake ★ Sydny Miner's Mexican Chocolate Pound Cake ★ Jill Weber's Apricot Brandy Sour Cream Pound Cake ★ Cardamom Coffee Cake ★ Sour Cream Poppy Seed Cake ★ Citrus Poppy Seed Cake ★ Frajil Farms Deceptive Yogurt Cake ★ Walnut Rum Spice Cake ★ Prune Sour Cream Coffee Cake ★ Cranberry Walnut Coffee Cake ★ Banana Streusel Coffee Cake ★

DESSERT, BUNDT, AND LAYER CAKES ★ 148

Buttermilk-Glazed Apple Cake Studded with Coconut and Walnuts ★ Banana Cake ★ Verdi's Double Lemon Cake with Fresh Lemon Zest Glaze ★ Dain Fritz's Grandmother's Carrot Cake ★ Rum-Spiked Pumpkin and Nut Cake ★ Classic Butter Cake ★ White Chocolate Cake ★ New England Maple Cake with Maple Frosting ★ Chocolate Babka ★ Jane P. Wilson's Never-Fail Chocolate Cake with Classic White Icing ★ Black Chocolate Cake ★ Coconut Cake with Coconut Syrup ★ Maxine Weinberg's Black-Bottom Cupcakes ★ Mocha Cupcakes ★

THE
BakeSale
Cookbook

★ QUINTESSENTIAL AMERICAN DESSERTS ★

Introduction

The first time that I ever baked anything for a bake sale was four years ago. I made Buttermilk-Glazed Apple Cake Studded with Coconut and Walnuts, one of my all-time favorites. It was for a bake sale/yard sale/fundraiser at the Russell Cooperative Preschool, attended by my then three-year-old daughter, Lauren. I delivered the cake at 8:00 A.M. and went home. When I returned at 10:00 A.M. for my two-hour stint staffing the tables, I discovered that my apple cake, cut into twelve individually wrapped pieces, was long gone. I was told that a man had purchased a cup of coffee and one piece of apple cake, and had sat down to relax at a nearby picnic table. After one bite, he got up and bought the remaining eleven pieces. Needless to say, I was compelled to track him down.

The apple cake, according to mystery man Mark Manning, was exactly the same as one made by his favorite grandmother for her church's bake sales. He wanted to savor the cake of his memory, relish the tastes, and re-create the feelings from his childhood.

Mark asked if he could buy three more cakes from me; I laughed and gave him the recipe. We became fast friends.

The BakeSale Cookbook literally came out of that experience: I wanted to re-create the past and produce a book that would be *the* book you turned to when you wanted to create an irresistible dessert for a bake sale/dinner party/birthday party, the book you turned to when you wanted to be a star (albeit not a showy star) and get the satisfaction I got from selling all twelve pieces of my apple cake to one person.

Bake sales, like yard sales, seemed, at one time, to be a dying, out-of-style tradition, but there are devotees for both, and both are making a comeback. (Even Martha Stewart featured bake sales in an issue of her magazine!) But you don't have to be baking for profit to use this collection of quintessential American desserts to delight family and friends.

For the past year, my children, Lauren and Benjamin, have been falling asleep to the sound of my steel-gray KitchenAid mixer whirring butter to creaminess, eggs to frothiness, and flour to smoothness. Hours later, my husband, Mark, and I would fall asleep to the sound of the dishwasher scrubbing the bowl of that very same KitchenAid, some other spoons and bowls, and a sheet, pie, or Bundt pan. I have baked at least one thing almost every night, and sometimes I have baked five things in a day. I have made cookies and pies that turned out perfectly the first time and have given up on bars and cakes that didn't work even after five valiant attempts. I retested up until the day I turned in the manuscript, even rejecting two cookie recipes at the last minute (almond macaroons and coconut macaroons that just didn't impress me enough).

Although I have always loved to bake, I have never considered myself a particularly skilled or brilliant baker. If I had any illusions to the contrary, they were immediately dispelled by the process of testing recipes for this book. I went through many stages. I was, at first, inspired and excited. I was eager to start the process, but the reality of finding recipes was, I admit, daunting. But then I met Rachel Travers, who told me that her mother, Bernice "Bercie" Travers, had been collecting recipes for years and years. She was sure, she said, that Bercie would share them with me. I called

Bercie, who welcomed me into her home and sent me back to mine with boxes of notebooks filled with recipes.

There were not only recipes for desserts but recipes for entrees, appetizers, side dishes, salads, drinks, and even a recipe for ridding closets of moths. Bercie had started listening to a radio food show in the late sixties and listened faithfully just about every day. She wrote down everything. Each recipe is dated and attributed to a caller, few of whom gave full names. Using those recipes, Bercie cooked in her home and sold her foodstuffs to fundraisers; she became a paid bake-sale contributor.

I had uncovered a buried treasure. The boxes were overflowing, thrilling, historical, hysterical, maddening, inspiring, and endless. They housed thousands of recipes and many (potential) books, and it was impossible for me to stop going through them. I was obsessed, and knowing I had to stop, I begged Rachel to take the boxes away.

Then I started baking. Bercie never made many of the recipes she had recorded, so when I tried these, I didn't have the benefit of her mistakes; I had to make my own. And with the discovery of great desserts came a few terrible duds. More often, however, the recipes were just short of what I wanted. Some simply needed a small amount of work to bring them up to my standards, but I discovered, to my great disappointment, that there were often little problems that I couldn't always fix. I decided that I was not the right person to be writing this book; I longed to quit.

But I had a contract, and I couldn't quit. Instead, I read a lot and enlisted the help of Paige Retus, baker extraordinaire, who looked at recipes and said things like, "You just need to lower/raise the oven temperature," or, "Add some chocolate chips/more orange zest/less sugar/more nuts," and, "Don't you think you need to butter/not butter/flour the pan?" Her commentaries, criticism, and advice seemed magically to transform many borderline recipes from just okay to extraordinary.

Before *BakeSale* I never paid attention to specific instructions. I thought that bakers were too regulated, too careful. When I baked, as often as not, I dumped everything together in one bowl. I didn't flour pans. I didn't wait for eggs to come to room temperature, and I didn't add them one by one. I didn't add the flour and liquid portions in parts. I certainly never, ever sifted anything. Now, having followed the rules and seeing what a difference they make, I continue to follow the rules. My cakes are moister and smoother, my piecrusts flakier, my crispy cookies crispier, and my chewy cookies chewier.

I learned (the hard way) that instructions are not for naught. So follow the instructions. I am (truly) no pro: if I can do it, so can you.

Two months after I turned in the manuscript for *The BakeSale Cookbook,* my seven-year-old daughter, Lauren, gave me the best reason in the world to have a bake sale. She established Kid2Kid, a nonprofit organization that arranges for frequently hospitalized children to give gifts and support to children who are presently in the hospital.

The goals of Kid2Kid are twofold. The first is to assist the givers: to help them cope with their own past (and possibly future) hospitalizations. By giving gifts, Lauren and children like her are able to walk into hospitals of their own volition and give of themselves, which helps to ease the personal anguish and isolation they feel as a result of repeated hospitalizations.

The second goal is to assist the receivers: Currently hospitalized children are nurtured by a visit from compassionate, generous children who share their experience and clearly see them rather than their illness.

Kid2Kid operates by receiving donations of time from children who have been frequently hospitalized. Kid2Kid welcomes financial donations and brand new toys. All donations are, of course, tax deductible.

For more information, you can contact us at kid-2-kid@juno.com. Remember to put in the dashes.

Essential Ingredients: Stocking Your Pantry and Refrigerator

Pantry

ALL-PURPOSE FLOUR

BAKING POWDER

BAKING SODA

BROWN SUGAR, DARK AND LIGHT

CAKE FLOUR

CHOCOLATE:

>   MILK CHOCOLATE

>   UNSWEETENED CHOCOLATE

>   UNSWEETENED COCOA POWDER

>   SEMISWEET OR BITTERSWEET CHOCOLATE

>   SEMISWEET CHOCOLATE CHIPS

>   WHITE CHOCOLATE

COCONUT, SWEETENED SHREDDED

CONFECTIONERS' SUGAR

KOSHER SALT

ROLLED OATS

SUGAR

VANILLA EXTRACT

VEGETABLE SHORTENING (FOR PIES)

GROUND CINNAMON

GROUND CLOVES

GROUND GINGER

POPPY SEEDS

Refrigerator

BUTTER, UNSALTED

EGGS

LEMONS

PEANUT BUTTER, SMOOTH AND CRUNCHY

PECANS

SOUR CREAM, FULL-FAT

WALNUTS

YOGURT, PLAIN FULL- OR LOW-FAT

Essential Equipment

I made almost everything in the book using a KitchenAid mixer (the biggest one), the most longed for and useful wedding present we received. Although I wanted it so that I could fulfill my fantasy that Mark and I would weekly make yeast bread, in reality I have never used it for any bread other than a quick bread. Of course, you can also use a hand mixer or a wooden spoon and a whisk; it will simply take a little more time. If you cook and bake with any regularity, a KitchenAid mixer is well worth the investment.

Equipment

FOOD PROCESSOR

KITCHENAID MIXER

Pots and Pans

I have always been a big fan of Kaiser La Forme bakeware, but now, many, many recipes later, I am a fanatic. Like the KitchenAid mixer, La Forme pans are pricey but worth it. Made of heavy-gauge steel, coated with nonstick inside and outside, the line includes a must-have bund (also called Bundt) pan, cake pans, springforms, cookie and jelly sheets, muffin tins, several sizes of loaf pans, and specialty pans. Cooking is even, cleanup is easy, and the pans have a five-year warranty. Their brochures suggest a finished cooking time of 10 percent less than that recommended in recipe directions. Although they suggest lightly buttering pans, it is not necessary to flour them, which means you won't have shadows on your cakes. In my instructions, sometimes I say to flour a pan, but that is assuming you don't have a La Forme.

BAKING SHEET WITHOUT SIDES, 18 X 12 X 1

BUNDT PAN

CAKE PANS, 9 INCHES

CUPCAKE TINS

LOAF PANS, 9 INCHES

PIE PANS, 9 INCHES

TUBE PAN

8-INCH-SQUARE PAN

12 X 9 X 2-INCH BAKING PAN

2-QUART SAUCEPAN

3-QUART SAUCEPAN

ASSORTED STAINLESS-STEEL OR PLASTIC MIXING BOWLS

ASSORTED GLASS OR CERAMIC MIXING BOWLS

1-, 2-, AND 4-CUP OVENPROOF GLASS MEASURING CUPS FOR
    LIQUIDS

MEASURING CUPS, HEAVY-GAUGE STAINLESS STEEL

MEASURING SPOONS, HEAVY-GAUGE STAINLESS STEEL

OVEN THERMOMETER

ASSORTED RUBBER SPATULAS

FLEXIBLE STAINLESS STEEL SPATULA AND AN OFFSET SPAT-
    ULA FOR FROSTING CAKES

ASSORTED WOODEN SPOONS

OXO VEGETABLE PEELER

XYLISS CAN OPENER

OXO FLOUR SIFTER (GREAT FOR CONFECTIONERS' SUGAR
    TOO)

STRAINER

COOLING RACKS

SHARP KNIVES, SERRATED AND SMOOTH

CUTTING BOARD (A GOOD RESILIENT ONE, WOOD OR
    ACRYLIC)

KITCHEN TIMER

WOODEN CITRUS REAMER

WHISKS OF MANY SIZES

CITRUS PEELER

LEMON ZESTER

PARCHMENT PAPER

WAX PAPER

ALUMINUM FOIL

PLASTIC WRAP

ZIPLOCS

TOOTHPICKS

SHOE BOXES

BOXES, ASSORTED SIZES

POTHOLDERS, DISHTOWELS

ESSENTIAL
EQUIPMENT

Cookies

I love to make cookie dough, and my husband loves having hot, right-out-of-the-oven cookies. Instead of baking a whole recipe of dough I almost always bake a dozen and form the remainder into a cylinder, which I freeze. I often have several logs in the freezer, which means that if I have guests (particularly young ones), I can have an assortment of cookies without doing any actual work (but getting lots of credit).

Most of the cookies in *BakeSale* can be formed into logs and then chilled, either in the refrigerator or in the freezer.

TO MAKE COOKIE LOGS

Roll the dough into a cylinder, cover with waxed paper or plastic wrap, and refrigerate for 20 minutes. Roll the cylinder again to ensure that it has a good, uniform shape. If you're going to freeze the dough, double-wrap it in plastic wrap. The dough will keep 4 to 5 days in the refrigerator and up to 3 months in the freezer. When ready to use, slice off thin rounds with the tip of a very sharp knife, place on the cookie sheet, and bake as usual. Frozen cookies may take a minute or two longer.

TO MAKE FESTIVE COOKIES

Purchase a varied selection of colored decorating sugars (sometimes called sanding sugar). Roll the edges of any log-formed cookies in the colored sugar. Or, lightly press the flat surface of the slice into the sugar until well coated. Or, coat the flat side with one color, then roll the rim in a contrasting color. Bake as usual. These will, as pal Lizzy Shaw attests, elicit many oohs and aahs.

TO MAKE PINWHEEL COOKIES

Chill the dough of cream cheese or brown sugar cookies and then roll out into a ¼- to ⅜-inch-thick sheet. Sprinkle the surface with a thin coating of crushed peppermint candy, chopped nuts, chocolate or rainbow sprinkles, or colored sugar. Roll the dough up like a jelly roll, cover with waxed paper or plastic wrap, and refrigerate for 20 minutes. Roll the cylinder again to ensure that it has a good, uniform shape. When ready to use, slice off thin rounds with the tip of a very sharp knife and place on the cookie sheet. Bake for the time suggested by the recipe.

To make black and white pinwheels using black cocoa cookies and cream cheese or brown sugar cookies: Chill the doughs. Roll out the doughs into sheets of equal size, ¼ inch thick. Top the light dough with crushed "goodies," as above. Top with rolled-out chocolate dough. Roll, slice, and bake, as above.

TO TRANSPORT COOKIES

Line a shoe box with wax paper, parchment paper, or aluminum foil, and "file" the cookies on their sides, like cards, or pile them in columns. Cover with aluminum foil or plastic wrap.

Nancy Olin's Chocolate Chip Cookies

When my husband, Mark, turned thirty, I gave a small surprise party and asked everyone to bring a batch of homemade chocolate chip cookies. Mark was a big devotee of his mother's cookies and an even bigger critic of mine. In truth, I was a big critic of mine, too, and as often as not they ended up in the trash, even when I followed the Toll House recipe to a tee. Mark was asked to blindly judge the cookies, and (aside from his mother's) these were the ones he liked best.

½ pound (2 sticks) unsalted butter, a little softer than room temperature

1 cup light brown sugar

¾ cup sugar

2 eggs, at room temperature

1 generous teaspoon vanilla extract

2 cups all-purpose flour

1 teaspoon kosher salt

¾ teaspoon baking soda

2 cups semisweet chocolate chips

1 to 2 cups toasted walnuts, pecans, or cashews, chopped (optional) (see note on page 28)

Preheat the oven to 340 degrees. ("You don't really have to measure this," says Nancy, "just set your thermometer between 325 and 350 degrees.") Lightly grease a cookie sheet and, if desired, line with parchment paper.

Place the butter and sugars in the bowl of a mixer fitted with a paddle and beat until smooth. Scrape down the sides of the bowl, add the eggs and vanilla, and mix until just combined, being careful not to overbeat. Scrape down the sides of the bowl, add the flour, salt, baking soda, chocolate chips, and, if desired, the nuts, and mix until everything is well incorporated.

Place tablespoonfuls 2 inches apart on the prepared cookie sheet and transfer to the oven. Bake until brown on the edges and soft in the middle, about 12 to 13 minutes. *Do not overbake.* For crisper cookies, cool on the cookie sheet. For softer cookies, cool for 2 minutes and then remove to a rack. Cool the cookie sheet between batches.

★ **YIELD: ABOUT 3–4 DOZEN**

COOKIES

Options:

OMIT THE SEMISWEET CHOCOLATE CHIPS AND INCREASE THE NUTS BY 1 CUP.

OMIT THE SEMISWEET CHOCOLATE CHIPS AND ADD 1 TABLESPOON GRATED ORANGE ZEST.

SUBSTITUTE 1 CUP SWEETENED OR UNSWEETENED SHREDDED COCONUT FOR 1 CUP SEMISWEET CHOCOLATE CHIPS.

VARY THE CHIPS: USE MILK CHOCOLATE, WHITE CHOCOLATE, AND/OR BUTTERSCOTCH.

INSTEAD OF SEMISWEET CHOCOLATE CHIPS, USE THE BEST-QUALITY BITTERSWEET CHOCOLATE, COARSELY CHOPPED.

SUBSTITUTE 1 CUP WHITE CHOCOLATE CHIPS AND 1 CUP DRIED CRANBERRIES FOR
THE SEMISWEET CHOCOLATE CHIPS.

ADD 1 TABLESPOON GRATED ORANGE ZEST.

★ ★ *Note:* To toast nuts: Preheat the oven to 300 degrees. On a rimmed cookie sheet, spread the nuts in a single layer. Bake until the nuts are lightly browned, about 15 to 20 minutes. Cool completely before using or storing in the freezer in an airtight container.

Walnut Chocolate Chip Cookies

Inspired by the nut flours made by The California Press, these cookies are truly to die for. When I bring them to a party, people ooh and aah. The California Press makes flour from walnuts, hazelnuts, pecans, almonds, and pistachios, and these can be ordered from Dean and Deluca at 800-221-7714 or by mail order directly from The California Press at 707-944-0343 in Yountville, California. The nut flours cost about $18.50 for a one-pound bag, very expensive but worth it. If you can't get their flour, simply place toasted nuts in a food processor and grind into a powder, stopping just before the nuts turn to butter.

½ pound (2 sticks) unsalted butter, at room temperature

¾ cup sugar

¾ cup light brown sugar

1 egg, at room temperature

1 teaspoon vanilla extract

1 cup rolled oats, ground to a powder if desired

1⅜ cups all-purpose flour

¼ cup nut flour or ¼ cup toasted walnuts or pecans, finely ground (see note on page 28)

1 teaspoon baking soda

1 teaspoon baking powder

1 teaspoon kosher salt

2 cups semisweet chocolate chips

2 cups toasted walnuts or pecans, coarsely chopped (see note on page 28)

Preheat the oven to 325 degrees. Lightly grease a cookie sheet and, if desired, line with parchment paper.

Place the butter and sugars in the bowl of a mixer fitted with a paddle and beat until smooth. Scrape down the sides of the bowl, add the egg and vanilla, and mix until just combined, being careful not to overbeat. Scrape down the sides of the bowl, add the oats, flour, nut flour or finely ground nuts, baking soda, baking powder, salt, chocolate chips, and nuts and mix until everything is well incorporated.

Place tablespoonfuls 2 inches apart on the prepared cookie sheet and transfer to the oven. Bake until brown on the edges and soft in the middle, about 12 to 13 minutes. Do not overbake. For crisper cookies, cool on the cookie sheet. For softer cookies, cool for 2 minutes and then remove to a rack. Cool the cookie sheet between batches.

★ YIELD: ABOUT 3–4 DOZEN

Black Cocoa Cookies

When my teenage nephews, Michael and Nadav Nirenberg, come to visit, I try to have these cookies waiting for their arrival. But if I don't, I'm safe because Michael loves to cook and is just as happy to whip up a batch himself. These slightly crisp, dark chocolate cookies can be made as is or, for true decadence, with the addition of white or dark chocolate chips.

Since these cookies are so dark, it can be hard to tell when they are done. It may take you a couple of batches to perfect the baking time. When in doubt, undercooking is better than overcooking. I like these best once they've cooled, but I seem to be in the minority.

COOKIES

½ *pound (2 sticks) unsalted butter, at room temperature*

2 cups sugar

2 eggs, at room temperature

1 tablespoon vanilla extract

2 cups all-purpose flour

1 cup unsweetened cocoa powder

1 teaspoon baking soda

½ *teaspoon baking powder*

½ *teaspoon kosher salt*

1 ½ cups toasted walnuts, pecans, or hazelnuts, chopped (optional) (see note on page 28)

Preheat the oven to 350 degrees. Lightly grease a cookie sheet and line with parchment paper.

Place the butter and sugar in the bowl of a mixer fitted with a paddle and mix until smooth. Scrape down the sides of the bowl, add the eggs and vanilla, and mix until just combined, being careful not to overbeat. Scrape down the sides of the bowl, add the flour, cocoa powder, baking soda, baking powder, salt, and, if desired, the nuts, and mix until everything is well incorporated.

Place teaspoonfuls on the prepared cookie sheet and transfer to the oven. Bake until the edges begin to firm up, about 12 to 13 minutes. *Do not overbake.* For crisper cookies, cool on the cookie sheet. For softer cookies, cool for 2 minutes and then remove to a rack. Cool the cookie sheet between batches.

★ **YIELD: ABOUT 5 DOZEN**

Cocoa Crinkles

This is the kind of cookie that has made *BakeSale* such a thrill to write. My editor sent me the recipe, and although I tried it willingly, it isn't something I would have otherwise made or eaten. But these cookies are, as she promised, wonderful: crispy on the outside and brownielike on the inside.

Although they can be stored in an airtight container, they will lose some of their crispness, which will make them more brownielike all over. These freeze well, and the dough will hold in the fridge a couple of days if you don't want to use it all at once.

¼ cup (4 tablespoons) unsalted butter, melted and cooled

½ cup unsweetened cocoa powder

1 cup sugar

2 eggs, at room temperature, lightly beaten

1 tablespoon vanilla extract

2 cups all-purpose flour

1 teaspoon baking powder

1 teaspoon baking soda

½ teaspoon kosher salt

Confectioners' sugar, for rolling

Place the butter and cocoa powder in the bowl of a mixer fitted with a paddle and beat until smooth. Add the sugar and mix well. Add the eggs and vanilla and beat until combined. Scrape down the sides of the bowl and gradually add the flour, baking powder, baking soda, and salt and mix until everything is well incorporated. Cover with waxed paper or plastic wrap and refrigerate at least 3 to 4 hours or freeze up to 2 weeks.

Preheat the oven to 350 degrees. Lightly grease a cookie sheet and line with parchment paper.

To form the cookies, break off small pieces and roll into 1½-inch balls (about 2 tablespoons of dough). Roll each ball in confectioners' sugar and place on the prepared cookie sheet, leaving at least 2 inches of room between the balls. Transfer to the oven and bake until the cookies are set, about 10 to 15 minutes. Cool the cookies on the cookie sheet for 5 minutes and then remove to a rack.

Repeat until all the dough is used.

★YIELD: ABOUT 24 BIG COOKIES

Lizzy Shaw's Chocolate Meringue Cookies

Although these cookies can be kept for a few days in an airtight container, they are, says Lizzy, "like heaven on earth when served a little warm. They will have a brittle, shiny exterior and a chewy, light, delicious interior, sort of like crunchy chocolate air."

The parchment paper is essential; aluminum foil doesn't work well and neither does greasing the cookie sheet.

5 ½ cups confectioners' sugar
4 heaping tablespoons unsweetened cocoa powder
2 cups coarsely chopped walnuts, pecans, or hazelnuts
Dash kosher salt
5 egg whites (about ½ cup)

COOKIES

Preheat the oven to 300 degrees. Lightly grease a cookie sheet and line with parchment paper.

Place the sugar, cocoa, walnuts, and salt in a large mixing bowl and mix to combine. Add the egg whites and mix until just moistened. Do not overmix.

Drop heaping tablespoonfuls onto the prepared sheet, about 1½ inches apart. Transfer to the oven and bake until crackly on top but shiny and wet looking in the cracks, about 15 to 20 minutes. As soon as the cookies are cool enough to handle, remove them from the parchment paper.

Variations:

ADD 1 TEASPOON TO 1 TABLESPOON GROUND COFFEE.

ADD ½ TEASPOON MINT EXTRACT OR 1 TO 2 TABLESPOONS CRUSHED PEPPER-
MINT CANDY.

ADD A LITTLE ROSE WATER, WHICH CAN BE FOUND IN SPECIALTY MARKETS.
"LET YOUR IMAGINATION RUN WILD," SAYS LIZZY.

★ YIELD: 3–4 DOZEN

THE
BakeSale
Cookbook

Oatmeal Raisin Cookies

When I first made these cookies I used the recipe from the Quaker Oats box. Instead of hand mixing, I threw all the ingredients in the food processor, resulting in ground oats and a finer-textured cookie. Everyone loved them and I couldn't make enough. This version varies ever so slightly from the recipe on the box, and grinding the oats is not essential.

½ pound (2 sticks) unsalted butter, at room temperature

1 cup dark brown sugar

½ cup sugar

2 eggs, at room temperature

1 tablespoon vanilla extract

1 tablespoon water

1¾ cups all-purpose flour

1 teaspoon baking soda

½ teaspoon kosher salt

2½ cups rolled oats, ground to a powder if desired

COOKIES

Preheat the oven to 375 degrees. Lightly grease a cookie sheet and, if desired, line with parchment paper.

Place the butter and sugars in the bowl of a mixer fitted with a paddle and mix until smooth. Scrape down the sides of the bowl, add the eggs, vanilla, and water, and mix until just combined, being careful not to overbeat. Scrape down the sides of the bowl, add the flour, baking soda, salt, and oats, and mix until everything is well incorporated. Add up to 2 cups optional ingredients, by hand, if desired.

Place tablespoonfuls on the prepared cookie sheet and transfer to the oven. Bake until brown on the edges and soft in the middle, about 12 to 13 minutes. Do not overbake. For crisper cookies, cool on the cookie sheet. For softer cookies, cool 2 minutes and then remove to a rack. Cool the cookie sheet between batches.

★ YIELD: ABOUT 5 DOZEN

Options:

ADD ANY OF THE FOLLOWING BUT DO NOT ADD MORE THAN 2 CUPS TOTAL.

2 CUPS SEMISWEET CHOCOLATE CHIPS, WHITE CHOCOLATE CHIPS, OR MILK CHOCOLATE CHIPS

1 CUP BUTTERSCOTCH CHIPS

1 CUP TOASTED PECANS, WALNUTS, OR ALMONDS, COARSELY CHOPPED (SEE NOTE ON PAGE 28)

1 CUP SWEETENED OR UNSWEETENED SHREDDED COCONUT OR A COMBINATION

1 CUP RAISINS AND 1 TEASPOON GROUND CINNAMON

1 CUP DRIED CRANBERRIES AND 1 CUP WHITE CHOCOLATE CHUNKS OR CHIPS

SUBSTITUTE ½ CUP FINELY GROUND PECANS, WALNUTS, OR ALMONDS FOR ½ CUP FLOUR

Ginger Ginger Gingersnaps

True to their name, these cookies are very gingery and very snappy. For those who do not live for ginger, the fresh and the candied ginger can be reduced or eliminated.

¼ pound (1 stick) unsalted butter, at room temperature

1 cup sugar, plus additional for rolling

1 egg, at room temperature

3 tablespoons dark molasses

1½ teaspoons vanilla extract

2 cups all-purpose flour

2½ to 3½ teaspoons ground ginger

1½ teaspoons baking soda

1 teaspoon ground cinnamon

¼ teaspoon kosher salt

2 teaspoons finely chopped or grated peeled gingerroot (optional)

5 to 6 tablespoons finely chopped candied ginger (optional)

COOKIES

Preheat the oven to 350 degrees. Lightly grease a cookie sheet and, if desired, line with parchment paper.

Place the butter and sugar in the bowl of a mixer fitted with a paddle and mix until smooth. Scrape down the sides of the bowl, add the egg, molasses, and vanilla, beating well and scraping down the bowl after each addition, and mix until light and fluffy. Add the flour, ground ginger, baking soda, cinnamon, and salt and mix until everything is well incorporated. Add the fresh and/or candied ginger, if desired.

To form the cookies, break off small pieces and roll into 1-inch balls. Roll the balls in the additional sugar and place about 2 inches apart on the prepared cookie sheet. Flatten each ball into a flat disk using a water glass or your hand. Alternatively, the batter can be formed into a log and the cookies sliced (see page 24).

Transfer to the oven and bake until the cookies begin to brown, about 15 to 17 minutes. Do not overbake. For crisper cookies, cool on the cookie sheet. For softer cookies, cool for 2 minutes and then remove to a rack. Cool the cookie sheet between batches.

★ YIELD: ABOUT 3–4 DOZEN

THE
BakeSale
Cookbook
★

Janet Richmond Condon's Hermits

Janet's son, Chip, rents an apartment from us. When he heard that I was writing this book, he informed me that I *had* to include his mother's recipe for hermits, a classic molasses spice cookie. Although I had never tasted a hermit (and truthfully never wanted to), I acquiesced because, well, you just have to know Chip: if he said his mother's hermits were great, you had to believe him. And now I do.

¾ cup solid vegetable shortening

1 cup sugar

1 egg

¼ cup molasses

2¼ cups all-purpose flour

2 teaspoons baking soda

1 teaspoon ground cinnamon

½ teaspoon ground ginger

½ teaspoon ground cloves

⅛ teaspoon kosher salt

½ cup raisins

½ cup chopped walnuts

For the egg wash:

1 egg yolk

1 tablespoon water

Preheat the oven to 375 degrees.

Place the shortening, sugar, egg, and molasses in the bowl of a mixer fitted with a paddle and mix until creamy. Add the flour, baking soda, cinnamon, ginger, cloves, and salt and mix until creamy and stiff. Scrape down the sides of the bowl. Add the raisins and walnuts and mix again. Place all the dough in walnut-sized clumps on a greased 12 x 18-inch baking sheet, top with waxed paper, and, using a rolling pin, roll until an even thickness.

To make the egg wash: Place the egg yolk and water in a small bowl and mix well. Using a pastry brush, brush the top of the dough with the wash. Transfer to the oven and bake until browned and shiny, about 10 to 12 minutes. Let cool 10 minutes and cut into 24 pieces, using a pizza cutter.

★ YIELD: ABOUT 2 DOZEN

Ben's Favorite Molasses Sugar Cookies

At four and a half, my son, Ben, is not a dessert eater, often choosing raspberries (his favorite) or a pear over something as special as chocolate cake. However, these cookies, which came out of pal Nancy Olin's former cookie exchange, really send him. They're dark, spicy, soft in the middle, and firm on the edges. I agree wholeheartedly with his choice.

¾ cup (1½ sticks) unsalted butter, at room temperature

1 cup sugar, plus additional for rolling

1 egg, at room temperature

¼ cup molasses

1 teaspoon vanilla extract

2 cups all-purpose flour

2 teaspoons baking soda

1 teaspoon ground cinnamon

½ teaspoon ground cardamom

½ teaspoon ground ginger

½ teaspoon kosher salt

COOKIES

Preheat the oven to 375 degrees.

Place the butter and sugar in the bowl of a mixer fitted with a paddle and mix until smooth. Scrape down the sides of the bowl, add the egg, molasses, and vanilla, beating well and scraping down before each addition, and mix until light and fluffy. Add the flour, baking soda, cinnamon, cardamom, ginger, and salt and mix until everything is well incorporated.

To form the cookies, break off small pieces and roll into 1-inch balls. Roll the balls in the additional sugar and place on an ungreased cookie sheet or line one with parchment paper. Alternatively, the batter can be formed into a log and baked in slices (see page 24).

Transfer the cookies to the oven and bake until they begin to brown, about 8 to 12 minutes. For crisper cookies, cool on the cookie sheet. For softer cookies, cool for 2 minutes and then remove to a rack. Cool the cookie sheet between batches.

★ YIELD: ABOUT 3–4 DOZEN

Brown Sugar Cookies

These cookies are the perfect crisp brown sugar cookie. One day I was getting ready to make Ben's Favorite Molasses Sugar Cookies (page 43) when I realized I had no molasses. I substituted brown sugar and now I don't know which cookie I prefer.

For a more gingerbread-like cookie, double the amount of spices.

¾ cup (1½ sticks) unsalted butter, at room temperature

1¼ cups brown sugar, plus additional for rolling

1 egg, at room temperature

2 cups all-purpose flour

2 teaspoons baking soda

½ teaspoon ground cardamom

½ teaspoon ground ginger

1 teaspoon ground cinnamon

½ teaspoon kosher salt

COOKIES

Preheat the oven to 375 degrees.

Place the butter and sugar in the bowl of a mixer fitted with a paddle and mix until smooth. Scrape down the sides of the bowl, add the egg, and mix until light and fluffy. Scrape down the sides of the bowl, add the flour, baking soda, cardamom, ginger, cinnamon, and salt and mix until everything is well incorporated.

To form the cookies, break off small pieces and roll into 1-inch balls. Roll the balls in the additional sugar and place on an ungreased cookie sheet or line one with parchment paper. Alternatively, the batter can be formed into a log and baked in slices (see page 24).

Transfer to the oven and bake until the cookies begin to brown, about 8 to 12 minutes. Do not overbake. For crisper cookies, cool on the cookie sheet. For softer cookies, cool for 2 minutes and then remove to a rack. Cool the cookie sheet between batches.

★ YIELD: ABOUT 3–4 DOZEN

Pecan Sugar Cookies

A bit like old-fashioned pecan sandies, these rich and nutty cookies truly melt in your mouth.

1 cup toasted pecans, finely ground (see note on page 28)

½ pound (2 sticks) unsalted butter, at room temperature

6 tablespoons granulated or confectioners' sugar

2 teaspoons vanilla extract

2 cups all-purpose flour

1 teaspoon kosher salt

¼ cup confectioners' sugar, for sprinkling

Preheat the oven to 350 degrees. Lightly grease a cookie sheet and, if desired, line with parchment paper.

Place the pecans, butter, sugar, vanilla, flour, and salt in the bowl of a mixer fitted with a paddle and mix until well combined. Roll into one big ball, cover with waxed paper or plastic wrap, and refrigerate until firm, about 1 to 2 hours.

To form the cookies, break off small pieces and roll into 1-inch balls. Place on the prepared cookie sheet and flatten each ball into a flat disk using a wet water glass or your hand.

Transfer the cookies to the oven and bake until they begin to brown, about 14 to 16 minutes. Cool for 2 minutes, remove to a rack, and sprinkle with the confectioners' sugar. Cool the cookie sheet between batches.

★ YIELD: ABOUT 3–4 DOZEN

Brown Sugar–Almond Shortbread

The brown sugar gives these sweet, nutty cookies a little bit more chew than traditional shortbread. A cold glass of milk is a necessity.

¼ pound (1 stick) unsalted butter, at room temperature

¾ cup dark brown sugar

¼ cup confectioners' sugar

1 cup all-purpose flour

½ cup almonds, finely ground

½ teaspoon kosher salt

Preheat the oven to 350 degrees.

Place the butter, sugars, flour, almonds, and salt in the bowl of a mixer fitted with a paddle and mix until smooth. Press into an ungreased 8 x 8-inch baking pan and pat or roll flat. Use a small bottle or jar as a rolling pin.

Transfer the pan to the oven and bake until the shortbread is just beginning to brown, about 40 minutes. Cool in the pan for 10 minutes and cut into 16 pieces.

★ YIELD: SIXTEEN 2-INCH-SQUARE PIECES

Hazelnut Shortbread

These cookies are heavenly and addictive.

½ pound (2 sticks) unsalted butter, at room temperature
½ cup sugar
½ cup light brown sugar
1 teaspoon vanilla extract
1 cup hazelnuts, finely ground (about ¾ cup ground)
2 cups all-purpose flour
1 teaspoon kosher salt

Place the butter and sugars in the bowl of a mixer fitted with a paddle and mix until smooth. Scrape down the sides of the bowl, add the vanilla and hazelnuts, and mix until light and fluffy. Scrape down the sides of the bowl, add the flour and salt, and mix until everything is well incorporated. The batter will seem too dry, but that's the way it's supposed to be.

To form the cookies, make one large log and lightly smash it down to make four sides so that it is a square column (if you were looking at it from above) rather than a round column. Cover with waxed paper or plastic wrap and refrigerate at least 2 hours or freeze up to 2 weeks.

Preheat the oven to 350 degrees.

With the tip of a very sharp knife, slice off thin rounds and place on an ungreased cookie sheet or one lined with parchment paper.

Transfer to the oven and bake until the cookies are lightly browned, about 12 to 14 minutes. Do not undercook these cookies; they will be too chewy. Cool for 2 minutes and then remove to a rack. Cool the cookie sheet between batches.

★ YIELD: ABOUT 3–4 DOZEN

Liz Micheels's Ginger Shortbread

Liz makes her shortbread the traditional way: in an 8 x 8-inch pan. I form the dough into a log and then cut off slices. If you want to prepare these shortbreads in the more traditional manner, bake the dough until it is just starting to get golden on the edges, about 20 to 22 minutes. Cut the cookies into squares while warm and let them cool in the pan. If you can't find ginger packed in syrup (available at specialty food shops), place 1 heaping tablespoon finely chopped candied ginger and 1 tablespoon hot water in a small bowl and set aside until the ginger is soft, about 5 minutes. Use instead of the cubes and the syrup.

¼ pound (1 stick) unsalted butter, at room temperature
½ cup sugar
1 cup all-purpose flour
3 cubes ginger in syrup, finely chopped
1 teaspoon syrup (from the jar)

COOKIES

Place the butter and sugar in the bowl of a mixer fitted with a paddle and mix until smooth. Scrape down the sides of the bowl, add the flour, and mix until incorporated. Scrape down the sides of the bowl, add the ginger and ginger syrup, and mix until everything is well incorporated.

To form the cookies, make one large log. Cover with waxed paper or plastic wrap and refrigerate at least 2 hours or freeze up to 2 weeks.

Preheat the oven to 350 degrees.

With the tip of a very sharp knife, slice off thin rounds and place on an ungreased cookie sheet or line one with parchment paper.

Transfer to the oven and bake until the edges are lightly browned, about 14 to 15 minutes. Cool for 2 minutes and then remove to a rack. Cool the cookie sheet between batches.

★ YIELD: ABOUT 3–4 DOZEN

THE
BakeSale
Cookbook
★

Cream Cheese Cookies

If you didn't know that there was cream cheese in these cookies, you'd think they were very good, very rich butter cookies.

The baked cookies and the raw dough freeze well.

½ pound (2 sticks) unsalted butter, at room temperature

4 ounces (½ large package) cream cheese, at room temperature

1 cup sugar

1 egg yolk, at room temperature

1 teaspoon vanilla extract

2½ cups all-purpose flour

¾ teaspoon kosher salt

COOKIES

Preheat the oven to 325 degrees.

Place the butter, cream cheese, and sugar in the bowl of a mixer fitted with a paddle and mix until smooth. Scrape down the sides of the bowl, add the egg yolk and vanilla, and mix to combine. Scrape down the sides of the bowl, add the flour and salt, and mix until everything is well incorporated.

To form the cookies, break off small pieces and roll into 1-inch balls. Place on an ungreased cookie sheet or one lined with parchment paper and flatten each ball into a flat disk using a wet water glass or your hand. Alternatively, these can be rolled: Chill the dough until firm, at least 2 hours, roll the dough ¼ to ½ inch thick, and cut with any shape cookie cutter. Carefully transfer to a baking sheet with a spatula.

Transfer to the oven and bake until golden brown, about 14 to 16 minutes. Cool for 2 minutes and then remove to a rack. Cool the cookie sheet between batches.

★ YIELD: ABOUT 3–4 DOZEN

THE

BakeSale

Cookbook

★

From the Night Kitchen's Bittersweet Chocolate Walnut Moons

I used to own a take-out shop in Brookline, Massachusetts, called From the Night Kitchen. We made only four kinds of cookies: chocolate chip, oatmeal, bittersweet chocolate moons, and walnut moons. (I just had to get that night theme in there.) These were a favorite with my customers and staff: densely chocolatey and nutty. Of course, you don't have to form them into moons.

¼ pound (1 stick) unsalted butter, at room temperature
¾ cup toasted walnuts, finely chopped (see note on page 28)
⅓ cup sugar
½ cup unsweetened cocoa powder
1 cup all-purpose flour
¼ teaspoon vanilla extract
Confectioners' sugar, for sprinkling

COOKIES

Place the butter, walnuts, sugar, cocoa powder, flour, and vanilla in the bowl of a mixer fitted with a paddle and mix until the dough just comes together. Cover with waxed paper or plastic wrap and refrigerate at least 2 hours or freeze up to 2 weeks.

Preheat the oven to 300 degrees.

To make crescent moons: form the dough into 12 balls and shape each into a crescent moon. To make full moons or regular round cookies, break off small pieces and roll into 1-inch balls. Flatten each ball into a flat disk using a wet water glass or your hand.

Place the shapes on an ungreased cookie sheet or one lined with parchment paper. Transfer to the oven and bake until golden brown, about 14 to 16 minutes for the crescents, about 15 to 20 for the full moons. Cool for 2 minutes and then remove to a rack and sprinkle with the confectioners' sugar. Cool the cookie sheet between batches.

★ YIELD: 12 LARGE CRESCENT MOONS OR ABOUT 36 LITTLE

FULL MOONS

THE

BakeSale

Cookbook

★

Peanut Butter and Jelly Drops

Nancy Olin's original recipe called for placing chocolate kisses in the center of these cookies, but filling the center with jelly instead seemed too good an idea to give up. These are not traditional peanut butter cookies; without the jelly they look like a classic sugar cookie and have a mild peanut butter flavor. With the jelly, they look like a classic jelly tot.

⅓ cup (5⅓ tablespoons) unsalted butter or stick margarine, at room
temperature
1 cup sugar, plus additional for rolling
2 eggs, at room temperature
¼ cup whole milk
5 heaping tablespoons peanut butter
2¼ cups all-purpose flour
2 teaspoons baking powder
⅛ teaspoon kosher salt
¼ to ½ cup grape, raspberry, or strawberry jam or 36 chocolate
kisses (optional)

COOKIES

Preheat the oven to 325 degrees. Lightly grease a cookie sheet and, if desired, line with parchment paper.

Place the butter and sugar in the bowl of a mixer fitted with a paddle and mix until smooth. Scrape down the sides of the bowl and add the eggs, one at a time, beating well and scraping down the sides of the bowl before each addition. Add the milk and peanut butter, beating well before each addition, and mix until smooth. Add the flour, baking powder, and salt and mix until everything is well incorporated. Cover with waxed paper or plastic wrap and refrigerate until the dough firms up a bit, about ½ hour.

To form the cookies, break off small pieces and roll into 1-inch balls. Roll the balls in the additional sugar and place on the prepared cookie sheet. If filling with jelly or chocolate kisses, use your thumb to gently push in the center of the ball, forming a small circle in the middle of the cookie.

Transfer to the oven and bake until just golden, about 15 minutes. If using kisses, immediately place a kiss in the center of the cookie, cool for 2 minutes, and then remove to a rack. If filling with jam, push the center down again, cool for 2 minutes, and then remove to a rack. When completely cooled, fill the center with jelly. Cool the cookie sheet between batches.

★ **YIELD: ABOUT 2½–3 DOZEN**

John Schaub's Peanut Butter Cookies

Years ago I was asked to come up with a recipe for peanut butter cookies and, without thinking, said yes. The problem is, I hate peanut butter so much I don't even like to be in a room where it's being consumed. So I begged my baker friend John for a recipe; he used to make dozens of these every day. I just never visited his shop during those hours.

½ pound (2 sticks) unsalted butter, at room temperature

1 cup sugar

1 cup light brown sugar

2 eggs, at room temperature

2 teaspoons vanilla extract

1½ cups smooth peanut butter

3⅓ cups all-purpose flour

1½ teaspoons baking soda

½ teaspoon kosher salt

¾ cup peanuts, coarsely chopped (optional)

COOKIES

Preheat the oven to 300 degrees. Lightly grease a cookie sheet and, if desired, line with parchment paper.

Place the butter and sugars in the bowl of a mixer fitted with a paddle and mix until smooth. Scrape down the sides of the bowl and add the eggs, vanilla, and peanut butter, beating and scraping down the bowl before each addition, being careful not to overbeat. Add the flour, soda, and salt and mix until everything is well incorporated. Add the peanuts, if using, by hand and stir well.

Place heaping teaspoonfuls on the prepared cookie sheet and flatten with the tines of a fork. If the dough is tacky, dip the fork tines in flour before you flatten the cookies. Transfer to the oven and bake until brown on the edges and soft in the middle, about 15 to 18 minutes. Do not overbake. For crisper cookies, cool on the cookie sheet. For softer cookies, cool for 2 minutes and then remove to a rack. Cool the cookie sheet between batches.

★ YIELD: ABOUT 3–4 DOZEN

THE
BakeSale
Cookbook
★

Sesame Seed Cookies

I've had this recipe since college, and I can no longer remember its source. The original used peanut oil instead of butter, but I just couldn't quite stomach it, not being a fan of peanut products. I press these down with a fork both ways so that unless you look very closely, they look like a classic peanut butter cookie. You can toast the sesame seeds and the coconut or not, as you prefer. These keep well and can be frozen either as dough or as cookies.

COOKIES

¾ cup (1½ sticks) unsalted butter, at room temperature

1 cup light brown sugar

1 egg, at room temperature

½ teaspoon vanilla extract

½ teaspoon almond extract

1¼ cups toasted sesame seeds

¾ cup lightly toasted unsweetened or sweetened shredded coconut, or a combination

2 cups all-purpose flour

1 teaspoon baking powder

1 teaspoon baking soda

½ teaspoon kosher salt

Preheat the oven to 350 degrees. Lightly grease a cookie sheet and, if desired, line with parchment paper.

Place the butter and sugar in the bowl of a mixer fitted with a paddle and mix until smooth. Scrape down the sides of the bowl and add the egg, vanilla, almond extract, sesame seeds, and coconut, stirring well and scraping down the sides of the bowl before each addition. Add the flour, baking powder, baking soda, and salt and mix until well incorporated.

To form the cookies, break off small pieces and roll into 1-inch balls and place on the prepared cookie sheet. Flatten the balls with the tines of a fork both ways to create a crisscross pattern. Transfer to the oven and bake until light golden, about 12 to 13 minutes. Cool for 2 minutes and then remove to a rack. Cool the cookie sheet between batches.

★ YIELD: ABOUT 4 DOZEN

Greek Cognac Cookies

A great classic butter cookie. If the cognac is not to your taste, simply substitute water or milk.

½ pound (2 sticks) unsalted butter, at room temperature
1 cup confectioners' sugar, plus additional for sprinkling
1 egg yolk, at room temperature
1 tablespoon cognac or brandy
2 cups all-purpose flour

COOKIES

Place the butter in a bowl of a mixer fitted with a paddle and mix until smooth. Scrape down the sides of the bowl, *gradually* add the sugar (or it will fly all over the place), and blend until well incorporated. Scrape down the sides of the bowl, add the egg yolk and cognac, and mix well. Scrape down the sides of the bowl, gradually add the flour, and mix until well combined. Cover with waxed paper or plastic wrap and refrigerate at least 3 to 4 hours or freeze up to 2 weeks.

Preheat the oven to 325 degrees.

To form the cookies, break off small pieces and roll into 1-inch balls. Place on an ungreased cookie sheet and transfer to the oven. Bake until very lightly browned, about 20 to 25 minutes. Cool for 2 minutes and remove to a rack. When the cookies have cooled, sprinkle with the additional confectioners' sugar. Cool the cookie sheet between batches.

★ YIELD: ABOUT 3–4 DOZEN

Jenny deBell's Snickerdoodles

This is the cookie that Jenny grew up on: her family made it for every holiday and after making them just once, I could see why. Jenny's suggestions: *don't* replace the margarine with all butter, and if you are a fan of cinnamon, bump up the quantity a little bit each time you make these cookies until you get just the right kick.

For the cookies:

½ pound (2 sticks) margarine, or ¼ pound (1 stick) margarine and
¼ pound (1 stick) unsalted butter, at room temperature

1½ cups sugar

2 eggs, at room temperature

2¾ cups all-purpose flour

2 teaspoons cream of tartar

1 teaspoon baking soda

½ teaspoon kosher salt

For the cinnamon sugar:

2 tablespoons sugar

2 to 4 teaspoons ground cinnamon

To make the cookies: Place the margarine and sugar in the bowl of a mixer fitted with a paddle and mix until smooth. Scrape down the sides of the bowl and add the eggs, one at a time, beating well and scraping down the sides of the bowl before each addition. Add the flour, cream of tartar, baking soda, and salt and mix until everything is well incorporated. Cover with waxed paper or plastic wrap and refrigerate at least 2 hours or freeze up to 2 weeks.

To make the cinnamon sugar: Place the sugar and cinnamon in a small bowl and mix to combine.

Preheat the oven to 400 degrees.

To form the cookies, break off small pieces and roll into 1-inch balls. Roll the balls in the cinnamon sugar and place on an ungreased cookie sheet.

Transfer to the oven and bake until just barely golden, about 8 to 10 minutes. For crisper cookies, cool on the cookie sheet. For softer cookies, cool for 2 minutes and then remove to a rack. Cool the cookie sheet between batches.

★ YIELD: ABOUT 3–4 DOZEN

COOKIES

Melting Moments

Another beauty from Jenny deBell's family. This old-fashioned cookie comes from her grandmother, Lois deBell. Although these cookies are somewhat dry, they melt in your mouth. I love them and find them hard to resist.

For the cookies:
½ pound (2 sticks) unsalted butter, at room temperature
⅓ cup confectioners' sugar
¾ cup cornstarch
1 cup all-purpose flour

For the glaze:
1 cup confectioners' sugar
1 tablespoon unsalted butter, at room temperature
1 tablespoon fresh lemon juice
1 tablespoon orange juice

To make the cookies: Place the butter and sugar in the bowl of a mixer fitted with a paddle and mix until smooth. Scrape down the sides of the bowl, add the cornstarch and flour, and mix until well combined. Cover with waxed paper or plastic wrap and refrigerate at least 3 to 4 hours or freeze up to 2 weeks.

Preheat the oven to 350 degrees. Lightly grease a cookie sheet and line with parchment paper.

To form the cookies, break off small pieces and roll into 1-inch balls. Place the balls on the prepared cookie sheet and flatten them with a wet water glass or your hand.

Transfer to the oven and bake until the cookies are just starting to color, about 10 to 12 minutes. Cool on the cookie sheet; the cookies are quite delicate.

To make the glaze: Place the confectioners' sugar and butter in a bowl and beat until smooth. Gradually add the lemon juice and orange juice and beat until smooth. Dab a little on each cooled cookie.

★ YIELD: ABOUT 2 DOZEN

COOKIES

Jam Thumbprint Cookies

When I was in college, I spent too much time baking and, I might add, eating cookies. These, adapted from *The Joy of Cooking,* were one of the reasons why.

½ pound (2 sticks) unsalted butter, at room temperature

⅔ cup sugar

1 egg yolk, at room temperature (save the white for rolling if using nuts)

1 teaspoon vanilla extract

2½ cups all-purpose flour

1 tablespoon ground cinnamon (or ½ teaspoon grated lemon rind)

½ teaspoon kosher salt

For rolling:

2 tablespoons sugar

1 teaspoon ground cinnamon

or

1 egg white

2 tablespoons finely ground toasted walnuts, pecans, hazelnuts, or almonds (see note on page 28)

½ cup raspberry, apricot, blueberry, blackberry, or peach jam

Place the butter and sugar in the bowl of a mixer fitted with a paddle and mix until smooth. Scrape down the sides of the bowl, add the egg yolk and vanilla, and mix until smooth. Scrape down the sides of the bowl, add the flour, cinnamon, and salt, and mix until everything is well incorporated. Cover with waxed paper and refrigerate at least 2 hours or freeze for 2 weeks.

Preheat the oven to 375 degrees. Lightly grease a cookie sheet and line with parchment paper.

To form the cookies, break off small pieces and roll into 1-inch balls. Roll the balls in the cinnamon sugar or in the egg white and ground nuts and place on the prepared cookie sheet. Transfer to the oven and bake for 8 minutes. Depress the center of the cookie with your finger or a rounded teaspoon and then return to the oven until just barely golden, about 5 minutes. Cool for 2 minutes and then remove to a rack.

When the cookies have cooled, fill each center with about 1 teaspoon of jam.

★ **YIELD: ABOUT 3–4 DOZEN**

COOKIES

Raspberry Linzer Cookies

T his is a favorite with kids and grown-ups alike.

½ pound (2 sticks) unsalted butter, at room temperature

1 cup sugar

1 teaspoon finely grated lemon zest

1 egg, at room temperature

1¼ cups all-purpose flour

1 cup toasted almonds, finely ground (see note on page 28)

½ teaspoon ground cinnamon

¼ teaspoon kosher salt

1 tablespoon unsweetened cocoa powder (optional)

1 cup raspberry, strawberry, or any red fruit preserve

Place the butter and sugar in the bowl of a mixer fitted with a paddle and mix until smooth. Scrape down the sides of the bowl, add the lemon zest and egg, and mix until well combined. Scrape down the sides of the bowl and add the flour, almonds, cinnamon, salt, and cocoa powder, if using. Form the dough into 2 disks, cover with waxed paper or plastic wrap, and refrigerate until firm, about 1 to 2 hours.

Preheat the oven to 350 degrees. Lightly grease a cookie sheet and line with parchment paper.

Lightly flour a work surface and roll out one disk to a ⅛- to ¼-inch thickness. Brush off any excess flour, and, using heart-shaped cookie cutters, make hearts of various sizes. Repeat with the remaining disk.

If desired, use a smaller cookie cutter to cut out the center of half of the hearts. Top the hearts with the same size heart frames. Apply a little bit of water with a small brush to make them adhere.

Place the double hearts on the prepared cookie sheet and transfer to the oven. Bake until just turning golden, about 10 minutes. Place the remaining hearts and heart frames on another cookie sheet and refrigerate.

Fill the center of the baked hearts with preserves and return to the oven for 2 minutes. Set aside to cool.

Transfer the single hearts to the oven and bake until golden, about 10 to 12 minutes. Cool for 2 minutes and then remove to a rack.

★YIELD: 2–4 DOZEN, DEPENDING ON THE SIZE OF YOUR
COOKIE CUTTERS

COOKIES

Options:

FOLLOW THE DIRECTIONS FOR JAM THUMBPRINT COOKIES ON PAGE 68.

MAKE HEART SANDWICHES: WAIT UNTIL THE COOKIES HAVE COOLED COMPLETELY, THEN COVER ONE HEART WITH JELLY AND TOP WITH ANOTHER HEART OF THE SAME SIZE.

Toffee

This is really a confection, but it's so good, I couldn't resist including the recipe here. It takes only minutes to make.

Store in the refrigerator or at room temperature in an airtight container up to 1 month.

½ pound (2 sticks) unsalted butter

1 cup sugar

3 tablespoons water

¾ to 1 cup semisweet chocolate chips

1 to 1½ cups chopped toasted pecans or walnuts (optional) (see note on page 28)

Lightly grease an 8 x 12-inch baking pan.

Place the butter, sugar, and water in a large heavy-bottomed skillet over medium-high heat and cook until the mixture comes to a low boil. Lower the heat to medium and cook, stirring constantly, until the mixture turns a cinnamon color with streaks of brown and reaches the hard-crack stage (when you drop a bit into cold water, it will form a brittle mass), about 7 minutes, or reaches about 300 degrees on a candy thermometer.

Immediately pour the candy into the prepared pan and let sit until just warm, about 5 minutes. Sprinkle with the chocolate, and, when the chocolate has melted, smooth down with a knife. Just before it has hardened, add the nuts, if using. Refrigerate until cold and then break into pieces.

Coconut Crackle Cookies

Susan Coe is Ben and Lauren's beloved preschool teacher. A macaroon hater but a coconut lover, she was cautious when I showed up with these. To her delight, they have the good qualities (coconut flavor, crunchy texture) of macaroons without, to her, the bad (chewy, mushy texture).

¼ pound (1 stick) unsalted butter, at room temperature

½ cup sugar

½ cup light brown sugar

1 egg, at room temperature

1 teaspoon vanilla extract

1 cup all-purpose flour

1 cup rolled oats, ground to a powder

*1 cup unsweetened or sweetened shredded coconut, or a combination,
ground to a powder*

1 teaspoon baking powder

¼ teaspoon baking soda

½ teaspoon kosher salt

*¼ cup unsweetened or sweetened shredded coconut, or a combination,
for rolling*

COOKIES

Preheat the oven to 350 degrees. Lightly grease a cookie sheet and, if desired, line with parchment paper.

Place the butter and sugars in the bowl of a mixer fitted with a paddle and mix until smooth. Scrape down the sides of the bowl, add the egg and vanilla, and mix until combined. Scrape down the sides of the bowl, add the flour, oats, powdered coconut, baking powder, baking soda, and salt and mix until everything is well incorporated.

To form the cookies, break off small pieces and roll into 1-inch balls. Roll the balls in the shredded coconut and place on the prepared cookie sheet. Transfer to the oven and bake until just barely golden, about 15 minutes. Let cool on the cookie sheet. Cool the cookie sheet between batches.

★ YIELD: ABOUT 3–4 DOZEN

Bars

When I first started catering, I hated making anything except bars and cookies because you can't just take a piece out of a cake in order to see how good it tastes without spoiling the look of your product. Bars allow you to sample, and they have great flexibility: they can be decorated, frozen, and cut to different sizes without spoiling the taste.

Butter crusts are used in many of the bar recipes. I considered making a master recipe, using only one crust for all, but since each recipe came from a different source, I decided to stay true to the originals. However, the crusts are interchangeable; if you have one that you particularly like, feel free to use that one.

TO TRANSPORT BARS

Line a box with wax paper, parchment paper, or aluminum foil, and place in single layers, separated by sheets of parchment paper. Cover with aluminum foil or plastic wrap.

All-American Brownies

The quintessential American brownie: chewy, a little underbaked, and amenable to as many changes and additions as you can think up. Nuts, M&Ms, coconut, Heath Bar chunks, chocolate chips (all kinds), and sprinkles can be mixed in or added on top.

½ pound (2 sticks) unsalted butter

4 ounces unsweetened chocolate, coarsely chopped

1¾ to 2 cups sugar

4 eggs, at room temperature

1 tablespoon vanilla extract

¾ cup all-purpose flour

½ teaspoon kosher salt

1 to 2 cups coarsely chopped toasted walnuts or pecans (optional) (see note on page 28); do not toast them if using on top

Preheat the oven to 325 degrees. Lightly grease and flour a 9 x 12-inch pan.

Place the butter and chocolate in a small saucepan over the lowest possible heat and cook until almost all the chocolate has melted. Off heat, stir until smooth and set aside to cool to room temperature.

Place the sugar and eggs in the bowl of a mixer fitted with a paddle and mix until thick and creamy. Add the vanilla and mix well. Scrape down the sides of the bowl, add the flour and salt, and mix until just combined. Do not overmix. Stir in the nuts, if desired. (Or sprinkle the nuts on top after you put the batter in the pan.)

Place in the prepared pan and transfer to the oven. Bake until a tester comes out clean, about 25 to 30 minutes. Cool in the pan and cut into 20 to 24 bars.

★ YIELD: ABOUT 20–24

BARS

Upstairs at the Pudding's Bourbon Brownies

These thick, rich, perfectly undercooked brownies are served at Upstairs at the Pudding, one of Cambridge's legendary restaurants. Rumor has it that when Goldie Hawn comes to town, she leaves with a batch of these. After making them just once, I knew why. My addition is the optional pecan topping.

¾ cup (1½ sticks) unsalted butter

4 ounces bittersweet or semisweet chocolate

3 eggs, at room temperature

1½ cups sugar

2 tablespoons bourbon

1 cup all-purpose flour

Pinch kosher salt

1 cup chopped pecans (optional)

Preheat the oven to 350 degrees. Lightly grease a 9-inch-square pan.

Place the butter and chocolate in a small saucepan over the lowest possible heat and cook until almost all the chocolate has melted. Off heat, stir until smooth.

Place the eggs and sugar in the bowl of a mixer fitted with a paddle and mix until thick and creamy. Add the bourbon and mix well. Add the chocolate mixture to the eggs and mix to combine. Scrape down the sides of the bowl, add the flour and salt, and mix until just combined. Do not overmix.

Spoon into the prepared pan and top with the pecans, if using.

Transfer the pan to the oven and bake until a tester comes out with a few crumbs attached, about 25 minutes. Cool in the pan and cut into 16 bars.

★ **YIELD: 16 BARS**

BARS

Double-Decker Chocolate and Coconut Brownies

Baking a great brownie is often to negotiate the fine lines of under-cooking, perfection, and overcooking. The temptation to undercook these brownies is great, but even slightly undercooking them makes them gummy. If you do undercook, they are great frozen, either alone or chopped up on vanilla or coffee ice cream.

¼ pound (1 stick) unsalted butter, at room temperature

1½ cups sugar

3 eggs, at room temperature

1 cup all-purpose flour

¾ teaspoon baking powder

½ teaspoon kosher salt

2½ squares unsweetened chocolate, melted

½ teaspoon vanilla extract

¾ cup unsweetened or sweetened shredded coconut, or a combination

Preheat the oven to 350 degrees. Lightly grease an 8 x 8-inch pan.

Place the butter and sugar in the bowl of a mixer fitted with a paddle and beat until smooth and fluffy. Add the eggs, one at a time, beating well and scraping down the sides of the bowl before each addition. Add the flour, baking powder, and salt and mix until everything is well incorporated. Place two-thirds of the mixture in a mixing bowl, add the chocolate and vanilla, and mix until thoroughly combined. Add the coconut to the remaining third and mix to combine.

Place the chocolate mixture in the prepared pan and smooth down with a knife. Top with the coconut mixture and smooth down with a knife. Transfer to the oven and bake until the top is just golden and a tester comes out clean, about 22 to 25 minutes. Cool in the pan and cut into 12 to 16 bars.

★ **YIELD: 12–16 BARS**

BARS

Engagement Brownies

For anyone who grew up eating Sara Lee chocolate cake, these brownies, neither too sweet nor too gooey, will bring back memories. I will forever call them "engagement brownies," because when my then future-father-in-law tasted them, he got down on his knees and proposed.

When Paige Retus, a self-described "registered nongoo eater," made them, she preferred them without the glaze and served them with ice cream. Her husband, Ted, a "registered goo eater," loved the glaze. Me? I'm sort of in between on the goo issue, but I do think the icing makes the brownie.

If you want, add nuts, M&Ms, coconut, sprinkles, chopped candy, or any other embellishment of your choice right after you add the glaze.

For the brownies:

5 tablespoons unsalted butter

6 ounces bittersweet or semisweet chocolate

2 eggs, at room temperature

¾ cup sugar

2 teaspoons vanilla extract

⅔ cup all-purpose flour

2 tablespoons unsweetened cocoa powder

½ teaspoon baking powder

¼ teaspoon kosher salt

For the glaze:

1 ½ teaspoons unsalted butter, at room temperature

1 teaspoon light corn syrup

⅓ cup confectioners' sugar

3 tablespoons water or prepared coffee

3 ounces unsweetened chocolate

1 teaspoon vanilla extract

Preheat the oven to 350 degrees. Lightly grease and line an 8 x 8-inch pan with parchment paper, allowing enough overhang to lift up the brownies.

To make the brownies: Place the butter and chocolate in a small saucepan over the lowest possible heat and cook until almost all the chocolate has melted. Off heat, stir until smooth. Set aside to cool to room temperature.

Place the eggs, sugar, and vanilla in the bowl of a mixer fitted with a whisk attachment and beat until lemon colored and thick. Add the flour, cocoa powder, baking powder, and salt and mix until just incorporated. Scrape down the sides of the bowl, add the cooled chocolate mixture, and mix until just combined. Pour into the prepared pan, smooth down with a knife, and transfer to the oven. Bake until the top is crackly and a tester comes out with a bit of crumb, about 20 to 25 minutes. Be careful not to overcook. Cool in the pan slightly and then carefully remove as a whole.

To make the glaze: Place the butter, corn syrup, sugar, and water in a small saucepan and bring to a boil over medium heat. Lower the heat to very low, add the chocolate and vanilla, and stir until smooth and glossy. Set aside to cool to room temperature.

After the brownies have cooled, spread with the glaze. Cut into 12 to 16 bars.

★ ★ *Note:* Of course you can add the glaze while the brownies are still in the pan, but you won't get any on the sides that way.

★ YIELD: 12–16 BARS

Cream Cheese Brownies

When I owned From the Night Kitchen, a take-out shop in Brookline, Massachusetts, we made cream cheese brownies every day. Here they are, slightly altered and even better.

For the cream cheese layer:

4 ounces cream cheese (½ package), at room temperature

1 egg yolk, at room temperature

1 teaspoon vanilla extract

2 tablespoons sugar

1 tablespoon all-purpose flour

For the brownie layer:

5 tablespoons unsalted butter

5 ounces semisweet or bittersweet chocolate

2 eggs, at room temperature

¾ cup sugar

½ cup all-purpose flour

1 teaspoon vanilla extract

½ teaspoon baking powder

¼ teaspoon kosher salt

½ to 1 cup semisweet chocolate chips (optional)

½ cup coarsely chopped nuts (optional)

Preheat the oven to 325 degrees. Lightly grease an 8 x 8-inch pan.

To make the cream cheese layer: Place the cream cheese in the bowl of a mixer fitted with a paddle and mix until smooth. Add the egg, vanilla, sugar, and flour, beating well and scraping down the sides of the bowl before each addition, and mix until creamy and well incorporated. Transfer to a mixing bowl and set aside.

To make the brownie layer: Place the butter and chocolate in a small saucepan over the lowest possible heat and cook until almost all the chocolate has melted. Off heat, stir until smooth. Set aside to cool to room temperature.

Place the eggs and sugar in the bowl of a mixer fitted with a paddle and beat until lemon colored and thick. Add the cooled chocolate mixture and mix until well combined. Scrape down the sides of the bowl, add the flour, vanilla, baking powder, salt, and the chocolate chips, if using, and mix until well combined.

Place half the chocolate mixture in the prepared pan, then dollop the cream cheese mixture over it, and don't worry if it doesn't cover it: it won't. Add the remaining chocolate mixture. Take a table knife and gently draw it from right to left and then from top to bottom, making a checkerboard pattern. Do not allow the mixtures to combine. Sprinkle with the nuts, if using.

Transfer to the oven and bake until the sides, but not the top, are just beginning to brown, about 25 to 30 minutes. Do not wait until a tester comes out clean: they are overbaked at that point. Set aside to cool for about 10 minutes, cut into 12 to 16 bars, cover, and refrigerate.

★ YIELD: 12–16 BARS

Peanut Butter Brownies

For those who favor the time-honored combination of peanut butter and chocolate, this brownie is a heavenly decadence.

For the peanut butter layer:

1 ounce cream cheese, at room temperature

3 heaping tablespoons smooth peanut butter

1 egg yolk, at room temperature

1 tablespoon sugar

1 tablespoon all-purpose flour

For the brownie layer:

5 tablespoons unsalted butter

5 to 6 ounces semisweet or bittersweet chocolate

2 eggs, at room temperature

¾ cup sugar

½ cup all-purpose flour

1 teaspoon vanilla extract

½ teaspoon baking powder

¼ teaspoon kosher salt

1 cup coarsely chopped peanuts

Preheat the oven to 325 degrees. Lightly grease an 8 x 8-inch pan.

To make the peanut butter layer: Place the cream cheese and peanut butter in the bowl of a mixer fitted with a paddle and mix

BARS

until smooth. Add the egg, sugar, and flour, beating well and scraping down the sides of the bowl before each addition, and mix until creamy and well incorporated. Transfer to a mixing bowl and set aside.

To make the brownie layer: Place the butter and chocolate in a small saucepan over the lowest possible heat and cook until almost all the chocolate has melted. Off heat, stir until smooth. Set aside to cool to room temperature.

Place the eggs and sugar in the bowl of a mixer fitted with a paddle and beat until lemon colored and thick. Add the cooled chocolate mixture and mix until well combined. Scrape down the sides of the bowl, add the flour, vanilla, baking powder, and salt and mix until well combined.

Place half the chocolate mixture in the prepared pan, then dollop the peanut butter mixture over it, and don't worry if it doesn't cover it: it won't. Add the remaining chocolate mixture. Take a table knife and gently draw it from right to left and then from top to bottom, making a checkerboard pattern. Do not allow the mixtures to combine. Sprinkle with the peanuts.

Transfer to the oven and bake until the sides, but not the top, are just beginning to brown, about 25 to 30 minutes. Do not wait until a tester comes out clean: they are overbaked at that point. Set aside to cool for about 10 minutes, cut into 12 to 16 bars, cover, and refrigerate.

★ YIELD: 12–16 BARS

Gretchen Taylor's Three-Layer Mint Brownies

When Gretchen Taylor started making these brownies, often called Grasshopper Squares, for her husband, Steve, New Hampshire's commissioner of agriculture, he was enraptured. Every Christmas his office has a cookie swap, and although he's supposed to come home with a little bit of everything, he always comes home with too many of these–he just can't stand to give them up.

The mint layer takes these brownies from superb to sublime, but if you don't like mint, you can substitute vanilla extract for the mint or omit the layer entirely. For holidays, Gretchen dresses up the mint layer with red or green food coloring.

For the brownie layer:

⅔ cup unsalted butter

3 ounces unsweetened chocolate

2 cups sugar

2 eggs, at room temperature

1 teaspoon vanilla extract

1½ cups all-purpose flour

1 teaspoon baking powder

½ teaspoon kosher salt

1 cup coarsely chopped nuts (optional)

For the mint layer:

¼ cup unsalted butter, at room temperature

2¼ cups confectioners' sugar

¼ teaspoon mint extract

4 tablespoons warm whole milk

For the frosting:

2 cups semisweet chocolate chips

2 tablespoons unsalted butter

Preheat the oven to 350 degrees. Lightly grease a 9 x 13-inch pan.

To make the brownie layer: Place the butter and chocolate in a small saucepan over the lowest possible heat and cook until almost all the chocolate has melted. Transfer the butter mixture to a large mixing bowl and add the sugar, eggs, and vanilla, stirring well and scraping down the sides of the bowl before each addition, and mix until smooth and glossy. Add the flour, baking powder, salt, and nuts, if using, scrape down the sides of the bowl, and pour into the prepared pan. Transfer to the oven and bake until a tester comes out clean, about 20 minutes. Set aside to cool.

To make the mint layer: Place the butter and sugar in a small mixing bowl and mix until smooth. Add the mint and milk and mix until smooth. It will seem very thin. Spread a thin layer on the cooled brownies.

To make the frosting: Place the chocolate chips and butter in a small saucepan over the lowest possible heat and cook until almost all the chocolate has melted. Off heat, stir until smooth. Drizzle over the mint layer. Cool for 1 hour and cut into 32 bars. (If you wait longer, the chocolate will crack.) Cover and refrigerate for the strongest, coolest mint sensation.

★ YIELD: 32 BARS

BARS

Rocky Road Bars

These bars are not for the faint of heart. While I wouldn't want to eat them on a regular basis, they definitely have a place on a bake-sale table. The original recipe, from Bercie's collection, calls for an unimaginable three cups of confectioners' sugar in the frosting. This version is a bit less sweet but still intense: my six-year-old daughter, Lauren, cut herself an average-sized piece and after eating a fourth of it asked if it would be OK if she took a little break.

For the first layer:

¼ pound (1 stick) unsalted butter

1 ounce unsweetened chocolate

1 cup sugar

2 eggs, at room temperature

1 teaspoon vanilla extract

1 cup all-purpose flour

½ to 1 cup coarsely chopped toasted walnuts, pecans, or peanuts (see note on page 28)

1 teaspoon baking powder

For the second layer:

6 ounces cream cheese, at room temperature

½ cup sugar

2 tablespoons all-purpose flour

¼ cup (4 tablespoons) unsalted butter, at room temperature

1 egg, at room temperature

½ teaspoon vanilla extract

¼ cup toasted walnuts, pecans, or peanuts, coarsely chopped (see note on page 28)

1 cup semisweet chocolate chips

2 cups mini marshmallows

For the frosting:

¼ cup (4 tablespoons) unsalted butter

1 ounce unsweetened chocolate

2 ounces cream cheese

¼ cup whole milk

1 cup confectioners' sugar

1 teaspoon vanilla extract

Preheat the oven to 350 degrees. Lightly grease and flour a 9 x 13-inch pan.

To make the first layer: Place the butter and chocolate in a small pan and cook over the lowest possible heat until almost all the chocolate has melted. Off heat, add the sugar, eggs, vanilla, flour, nuts, and baking powder and mix well. Press into the prepared pan and set aside.

To make the second layer: Place the cream cheese, sugar, flour, butter, egg, and vanilla in the bowl of a mixer fitted with a paddle and mix until smooth and fluffy. Scrape down the sides of the bowl, add the nuts, mix to combine, and spread over the first layer. Sprinkle with the chocolate chips and transfer to the oven. Bake until slightly golden on the edges, about 20 to 25 minutes.

Sprinkle the second layer with the marshmallows and return the pan to the oven until the marshmallows are just melted but not colored, about 3 minutes.

To make the frosting: Place the butter and chocolate in a small pan and cook over the lowest possible heat until almost all the chocolate has melted. Add the cream cheese and milk and mix until smooth. Add the confectioners' sugar and vanilla and mix until smooth. Immediately pour the frosting over the marshmallows and briefly swirl the two mixtures together. Cool in the pan and cut into 36 to 48 bars. Cover and refrigerate.

★ YIELD: 36–48 BARS

Shirley's Chocolate Pecan Bourbon Bars

Although these bars, from Bercie's collection, look like a brownie with a butter crust, their taste is reminiscent of a not-so-sweet, slightly boozy pecan pie. I have made the cinnamon optional because, although I am a huge fan of cinnamon, I prefer these bars without it. However, I was outnumbered by my critics. If in doubt, it is better to slightly underbake these bars.

For the crust:

1¼ cups all-purpose flour

½ teaspoon baking powder

¼ cup sugar

½ teaspoon ground cinnamon (optional)

¼ pound (1 stick) unsalted butter, cold and cut into small pieces

1 cup finely chopped toasted pecans (see note on page 28)

For the filling:

¼ cup (4 tablespoons) unsalted butter

1 ounce semisweet chocolate

3 eggs, at room temperature

1¼ cups brown sugar

2 tablespoons bourbon

1 teaspoon vanilla extract

1 cup coarsely chopped pecans (not toasted)

Preheat the oven to 350 degrees.

To make the crust: Place the flour, baking powder, sugar, and cinnamon, if using, in a bowl of a food processor fitted with a steel blade and process until combined. While the processor is running, add the butter and process until it resembles cornmeal. Add the nuts and process until the mixture just comes together. Press into a 9 x 13-inch pan and transfer to the oven. Bake until lightly colored but not golden, about 10 to 12 minutes. Set aside.

To make the filling: Place the butter and chocolate in a small pan and cook over the lowest possible heat until almost all the chocolate has melted. Off heat, stir until the mixture is smooth. Set aside to cool.

Place the eggs, sugar, bourbon, and vanilla in a small mixing bowl and mix until well combined. Add the cooled chocolate mixture, stir to combine, and pour over the crust. Top with the pecans and carefully transfer to the oven; the mixture will be very soupy. Bake until the top is brownielike, about 15 to 20 minutes. Cool in the pan and cut into 16 to 24 bars.

★ YIELD: 16–24 BARS

Pecan Turtle Bars

Rich, sticky, and absolutely divine.

For the crust:

1½ cups all-purpose flour

¾ cup brown sugar

¾ cup unsalted butter, at room temperature

1 cup coarsely chopped pecans

For the caramel layer:

¼ cup (4 tablespoons) unsalted butter

¾ cup brown sugar

½ teaspoon kosher salt

1 cup coarsely chopped pecans

¾ cup bittersweet chocolate, melted

Preheat the oven to 350 degrees.

To make the crust: Place the flour and sugar in the bowl of a food processor fitted with a steel blade and process until combined. While the processor is running, add the butter and process until smooth. Add the pecans and process until the mixture comes together. Press into a 9 x 13-inch pan and bake until dry to the touch but not yet colored, about 15 minutes.

To make the caramel: Place the butter, sugar, and salt in a pan and bring to a boil over medium-high heat. After it comes to a boil and the entire surface is coated with bubbles, cook for 1 minute, stirring continuously. Off heat, add the pecans and stir until well coated. Pour over the crust and push the pecans around so that they are evenly distributed. Transfer to the oven and bake until the caramel is bubbly, about 18 to 20 minutes. Cool to room temperature and then drizzle the chocolate over the top. Set aside to cool and then cut into 24 bars.

★ YIELD: 24 BARS

Chocolate Coconut Bars

Chocolate crust, coconut and nut filling, and chocolate on top—these bars, one of Bercie's, remind me of the coconut patties you see for sale in Florida. The melted chocolate can be sprinkled with chopped nuts, sprinkles, toasted coconut, M&Ms, or anything else you can think of.

For the crust:

1 ounce unsweetened chocolate

1 cup all-purpose flour

½ cup confectioners' sugar

½ teaspoon kosher salt

¼ pound (1 stick) unsalted butter, cold and cut into small pieces

For the filling:

1 can (14 ounces) sweetened condensed milk

1 cup unsweetened or sweetened shredded coconut, or a combination

½ cup chopped toasted walnuts or pecans (see note on page 28)

½ cup semisweet chocolate chips

Preheat the oven to 350 degrees. Lightly grease an 8 x 8-inch pan.

To make the crust: Place the chocolate in a double boiler over medium-high heat and cook until the chocolate has almost melted. Off heat, stir until smooth. Set aside to cool to room temperature but do not let it harden.

Place the flour, sugar, and salt in a food processor and process until combined. Add the butter, little by little, and process until it has the consistency of coarse cornmeal or is pebbly. Add the cooled chocolate and mix until thoroughly combined. Press into the prepared pan and transfer to the oven. Bake until just golden, about 12 to 15 minutes. Set aside.

To make the filling: Place the milk, coconut, and nuts in a bowl and mix to combine. Spread over the crust, transfer to the oven, and bake until lightly golden, about 20 to 25 minutes. Immediately sprinkle the chocolate chips over the filling, top with a tent of aluminum foil, and set aside for 5 minutes. Remove the foil tent and spread the melted chips evenly. Cool in the pan and cut into 16 bars.

★ YIELD: 16 BARS

Butterscotch–White Chocolate Brownies

While it's tempting to eat these right out of the oven, their taste improves as they cool. Before I made these I had never had a butterscotch brownie; when I read Bercie's recipe, I was curious enough to try them. They are heavenly and very, very rich so cut them into small pieces.

You can substitute semisweet chocolate for the white chocolate. Do not increase the amount of nuts: it will make the brownies too greasy.

¼ pound (1 stick) unsalted butter, at room temperature

1 cup light brown sugar

2 eggs, at room temperature

1 teaspoon vanilla extract

1 cup plus 2 tablespoons all-purpose flour

2 teaspoons baking powder

1 teaspoon kosher salt

1 cup finely chopped toasted pecans (do not use more) (see note on page 28)

1½ cups (about 5 to 6 ounces) finely chopped white chocolate

Preheat the oven to 325 degrees. Lightly grease a 9 x 13-inch pan.

Place the butter and sugar in the bowl of a mixer fitted with a paddle and mix until creamy. Add the eggs, one at a time, beating well and scraping down the sides of the bowl after each addition. Add the vanilla. Add the flour, baking powder, and salt and mix to combine. Scrape down the sides of the bowl, add the pecans and white chocolate, and mix until just combined: it will be thick and lumpy, almost like cookie batter.

Place in the prepared pan and transfer to the oven. Bake until the top is lightly golden and a tester comes out clean, about 25 minutes. Cool in the pan and cut into 32 bars.

★ YIELD: 32 BARS

Aunt Suzy's Chocolate Chip Gooey Bars

Jenny deBell's Aunt Suzy made these exceptional bars. For me, their gooey intensity makes them taste better after they've cooled, but my friend Gordon Benett likes them steaming hot–right out of the oven. He describes them, smirking, as "orgasmic."

If you can find a professional half-sheet pan (12 x 18 inches) you can make a slightly less sweet and thinner bar; simply reduce the baking time to 18 to 20 minutes. This will yield about 48 bars. Of course, you can also halve the recipe and use the size pan suggested in the recipe.

One recipe of Nancy Olin's Chocolate Chip Cookies dough makes a little over 3 pounds of dough (without nuts). One recipe of these bars uses a little over 2 pounds, so make the whole batch of dough and use the leftover pound for cookies. If you're not using premade dough, make the top layer of the bars first.

2 pounds chocolate chip cookie dough (page 26)
2 cups (12 ounces) semisweet chocolate chips
1 can (14 ounces) Eagle Brand sweetened condensed milk (the only brand Aunt Suzy would use)
2 teaspoons vanilla extract

Preheat the oven to 350 degrees. Lightly grease a 9 x 13-inch pan.

Spread half the cookie dough in the prepared pan.

Place the chocolate chips and condensed milk in a double boiler and cook, stirring occasionally, until the chips have melted and the mixture has thickened somewhat, about 3 to 5 minutes. Set aside to cool. Add the vanilla and mix to combine.

Spread the cooled mixture over the cookie dough and dollop the remaining cookie dough on top. Transfer to the oven and bake until lightly browned, about 20 to 25 minutes.

Let cool slightly and cut into 32 bars.

★YIELD: 32 BARS

Melanie's Grandma's Kansas Rhubarb Shortbread

If I saw these in a cookbook I would definitely pass them over. However, my friend Sarah Conover sent me the recipe, and since she has great instincts when it comes to cooking, I made them the very day the recipe came in the mail. I just happened to have rhubarb in the house, and when they came out of the oven, I devoured a third of the batch. In tiny slices. Standing up.

For the shortbread:
¼ pound (1 stick) unsalted butter, at room temperature
1 cup all-purpose flour, or ½ cup flour and 1 cup rolled oats
5 tablespoons confectioners' sugar
½ teaspoon kosher salt.

For the topping:
2 eggs, lightly beaten
¼ cup all-purpose flour
¾ teaspoon kosher salt
1½ cups sugar
2 cups diced rhubarb

Preheat the oven to 350 degrees.

To make the shortbread: Place the butter, flour, sugar, and salt in the bowl of a mixer fitted with a paddle and mix until it comes together. Press into an 8 x 8-inch pan and transfer to the oven. Bake until the edges are just beginning to brown, about 15 to 18 minutes.

To make the topping: Place all the ingredients in a medium-size bowl and mix until everything is completely incorporated. It will have a slightly gluey texture, but have no fear; you are doing it right.

Place the topping on the shortbread and transfer to the oven. Bake until the topping is set and just beginning to turn golden, about 35 to 45 minutes. Cool in the pan and cut into 12 to 16 bars.

Variation:

STRAWBERRY RHUBARB SHORTBREAD: SUBSTITUTE 1 CUP DICED STRAWBERRIES FOR ½ CUP RHUBARB.

★ **YIELD: 12–16 BARS**

Sesame Apricot Bars

A relic from my college cooking days, this slightly chewy, slightly crunchy bar is reminiscent of a sesame seed granola bar. Although the original recipe calls for raisins, because I am not a fan of cooked raisins I usually make substitutions. In addition, the apricots can also be replaced with any combination of dried cranberries, blueberries, cherries, dates, figs, prunes, or cherries.

¾ cup (1½ sticks) unsalted butter, at room temperature

1 cup light brown sugar

1 egg, at room temperature

1 cup all-purpose flour

1 cup rolled oats

½ teaspoon baking soda

½ teaspoon ground cinnamon

½ teaspoon kosher salt

1 cup finely chopped dried apricots

½ cup raisins

½ cup toasted sesame seeds (see note on page 28)

BARS

Preheat the oven to 350 degrees. Lightly grease a 9 x 13-inch pan.

Place the butter and sugar in a food processor fitted with a steel blade or a mixer fitted with a paddle and mix until smooth. Add the egg and mix well. Scrape down the sides of the bowl, add the flour, oats, baking soda, cinnamon, and salt, and mix to combine. Scrape down the sides, add the apricots, raisins, and sesame seeds, and mix until everything is well incorporated. Place in the prepared pan and spread evenly. Transfer to the oven and bake until golden brown, about 25 minutes. Cool in the pan and cut into 24 bars.

★ YIELD: 24 BARS

Coconut Toffee Bars

This bar is great for someone who likes chocolate but doesn't want the overload you get from brownies and other chocolate-based bars.

For the crust:

¼ pound (1 stick) unsalted butter, at room temperature

1 cup all-purpose flour

½ cup light brown sugar

½ teaspoon kosher salt

For the topping:

2 large eggs, at room temperature

1 cup light brown sugar

1 cup unsweetened or sweetened shredded coconut or a combination

1 cup chopped sliced almonds

1 teaspoon grated lemon zest (optional if using chocolate)

1 teaspoon vanilla extract

½ teaspoon kosher salt

1 cup semisweet chocolate chips (optional)

Preheat the oven to 350 degrees.

To make the crust: Place the butter, flour, sugar, and salt in the bowl of a mixer fitted with a paddle and mix until it comes together

Press into a 9 x 13-inch pan and transfer to the oven. Bake until the edges are just beginning to color, about 12 to 13 minutes.

To make the topping: Place the eggs, sugar, coconut, almonds, lemon zest, if using, vanilla, and salt in the bowl of a mixer fitted with a paddle and mix until the ingredients just come together. Do not overmix. Place the chocolate chips, if using, over the crust and then pour the topping over the crust. Transfer to the oven and bake until golden and set, about 20 to 25 minutes. Cool in the pan and cut into 24 to 32 bars.

★ **YIELD: 24–32 BARS**

Lemon-Glazed Pecan and Coconut Squares

Although I had been making these sweet, tart squares for years, when my friend Bob Raives sent me the Rolls-Royce of lemon zesters, I discovered a newfound joy in their creation. The zester (from Lee Valley Tools in Ottawa, Canada; 800-871-8158) is really a piece of woodworking hardware, but I couldn't stop cooking with the skinny shreds of citrus it produces.

For the crust:

1½ cups all-purpose flour

3 tablespoons sugar

½ teaspoon kosher salt

¼ pound (1 stick) unsalted butter

For the pecan and coconut filling:

3 eggs, at room temperature

1 cup dark brown sugar

1 cup chopped toasted pecans (see note on page 28)

¾ cup unsweetened or sweetened shredded coconut, or a combination

1½ teaspoons vanilla extract

For the lemon glaze:

½ cup confectioners' sugar

¼ cup fresh lemon juice

2 teaspoons grated lemon zest

Preheat the oven to 350 degrees. Lightly grease a 9 x 12-inch baking pan.

To make the crust: Place the flour, sugar, salt, and butter in the bowl of a mixer fitted with a paddle or a food processor fitted with a steel blade and mix until powderlike and well combined.

Pat into the prepared pan, transfer to the oven, and bake until just golden, about 15 minutes. Set aside to cool to room temperature.

To make the filling: Place the eggs, sugar, pecans, coconut, and vanilla in a mixing bowl and combine well. Pour over the crust, transfer to the oven, and bake until slightly browned, about 15 to 25 minutes.

To make the glaze: Place the confectioners' sugar, lemon juice, and zest in a small bowl and mix to combine. Brush over the bars while they are still in the pan and warm.

Cut into 24 bars with a very sharp knife and serve warm or at room temperature.

★ **YIELD: 24 BARS**

Amy Bodiker's Lemon Bars

Until I ate these, I had never met a lemon bar I liked; they were never lemony enough and too spongelike in consistency. I had given up on lemon bars until Amy Bodiker gave me the recipe for these smooth, tart bars. But be careful, it turns out that overcooking causes that nasty sponge-like texture.

For the crust:

1 cup all-purpose flour

½ cup confectioners' sugar, plus additional for sprinkling

Pinch kosher salt

¼ pound (1 stick) unsalted butter, cold and cut in small pieces

For the filling:

2 eggs, at room temperature

1 cup sugar

2 tablespoons all-purpose flour

¼ teaspoon kosher salt

Finely grated zest of 1 lemon

¼ cup fresh lemon juice (about 1 to 2 lemons)

BARS

Preheat the oven to 350 degrees. Lightly butter an 8 x 8-inch baking pan.

To make the crust: Place the flour, confectioners' sugar, and salt in a large bowl of a food processor fitted with a steel blade and mix to combine. Add the butter, a little at a time, and mix until the butter is completely incorporated. Press into the prepared baking pan and transfer to the oven. Bake until slightly golden, about 18 to 20 minutes. Set aside.

To make the filling: Place the eggs, sugar, and flour in a small bowl and mix to combine. Add the salt, lemon zest, and lemon juice and mix until completely incorporated. Pour over the crust and transfer to the oven. Bake until the filling is just set and beginning to turn golden, about 15 to 18 minutes. Do not overcook. Cool to room temperature and then refrigerate for at least 1 hour. Cut into 16 to 20 pieces and sprinkle with confectioners' sugar.

★ **YIELD: 16–20 BARS**

Eleanor Rashkind's Toffee Squares

Eleanor Rashkind of Virginia Beach, Virginia, gave this recipe to her daughter-in-law's niece, Jenny deBell, who gave it to me. The original recipe calls for melting the chocolate in a pot, but I didn't want to dirty another pot so I just return the whole thing to the oven for a minute or two.

½ pound (2 sticks) unsalted butter, at room temperature

1 cup light brown sugar

1 egg yolk

1 teaspoon vanilla extract

2 cups all-purpose flour

½ pound (2 cups) milk chocolate, well chopped

1 cup chopped toasted walnuts or pecans (see note on page 28)

Preheat the oven to 350 degrees. Lightly butter a 9 x 13-inch pan.

Place the butter and sugar in a bowl and blend until creamy and light colored. Add the egg yolk, vanilla, and flour, blending well and scraping down the sides of the bowl after each addition.

Spread into the prepared pan and pat down with your hands or a small rolling pin. Transfer to the oven and bake until golden brown, about 15 to 20 minutes. Spread the chocolate over the warm batter and let sit for 3 to 5 minutes. Sprinkle with the nuts.

Cut when warm into 24 pieces with a knife dipped in cold water.

★ YIELD: 24 BARS

Barbara Haber's Rugelach

Barbara Haber, the curator of books at Radcliffe College's Schlesinger Library, spends a huge amount of time researching food, but she didn't have to dig too far to find this family recipe. The origin of this pastry, says Barbara, is probably Austrian: at the end of the eighteenth century bakers celebrated the end of the Turkish siege by creating baked goods in the shape of crescents, a symbol found on the Turkish flag. Later, Americans added cream cheese to make the yeast-raised crescent more rich and pastrylike.

Because Jewish dietary law requires that no food containing dairy be served at a meal that contains meat, rugelach, which contains butter, sour cream, and cream cheese, was probably served at breakfast, after a vegetarian meal, or late in the evening, at least three hours after a meat meal.

For the pastry:

¼ pound (1 stick) unsalted butter, cold

½ cup sour cream (do not use low fat or nonfat)

4 ounces cream cheese (do not use low fat or nonfat)

1½ cups all-purpose flour

For the filling:

⅓ cup sugar

2 teaspoons ground cinnamon

1 egg, at room temperature

1 tablespoon water

2 tablespoons unsalted butter, melted

⅔ cup finely chopped toasted walnuts (see note on page 28)

Place the butter in a food processor fitted with a steel blade and process until creamed. Add the sour cream and cream cheese and process until creamed. Add the flour and mix until it just forms a soft ball. Divide into two balls, cover with plastic wrap, and refrigerate at least 3 hours and up to overnight.

Preheat the oven to 350 degrees. Lightly grease or line a cookie sheet with parchment paper.

Place the sugar and cinnamon in a small bowl and mix to combine. Set aside. Place the egg and water in a small bowl and mix to combine. Set aside.

Flour the work surface and place the balls, one at a time, on the surface. Roll out each ball with a floured rolling pin, to a 10- to 12-inch-diameter, ⅛- to ¼-inch-thick circle. (Alternatively, you can roll the balls in sugar for a sweeter treat and a messier process.) Brush each circle with half the melted butter. Sprinkle one-fourth of the cinnamon sugar and half the walnuts over each circle. Using a sharp knife or a pizza cutter, cut each circle into 12 to 16 wedges. Beginning at the wide end, roll up each wedge to form a crescent and place on the cookie sheet. Repeat until all the dough has been used.

Brush the tops with the egg mixture and sprinkle with the remaining cinnamon sugar. Transfer to the oven and bake until they are golden brown, about 30 minutes. Transfer to a wire rack to cool.

★ YIELD: 12–16

Apple Kuchen

These bars should be made by patient bakers with a bit of time because they look best when the apples are lined up in neat columns. This is not to say that it makes any difference in the way they taste.

For the crust:

2 cups all-purpose flour

½ cup sugar

¼ teaspoon kosher salt

½ teaspoon vanilla extract

½ pound (2 sticks) unsalted butter, cold and cut into pieces

For the filling:

1 pound cream cheese, at room temperature

¾ cup sugar

1 teaspoon vanilla extract

1 egg, at room temperature

For the topping:

2 tablespoons sugar

1½ teaspoons ground cinnamon

3 Granny Smith apples, peeled, if desired, cored, and thinly sliced

Preheat the oven to 450 degrees. Lightly grease and flour a 9 x 13-inch pan.

To make the crust: Place the flour, sugar, and salt in a large bowl or food processor fitted with a steel blade and mix to combine. Add the vanilla and butter, a little at a time, and mix until it resembles cornmeal. Press into the prepared baking pan and transfer to the oven. Bake until slightly golden but not brown, about 12 to 15 minutes. Set aside to cool.

Lower the oven temperature to 400 degrees.

To make the filling: Place the cream cheese, sugar, and vanilla in the bowl of a mixer fitted with a paddle and beat until creamy. Add the egg, mix to combine, and pour over the cooled crust.

Place the sugar and cinnamon in a small bowl and mix to combine.

Place the apples on top of the filling in two or three columns. Sprinkle with the cinnamon sugar and transfer to the oven. Bake until firm and a rich brown, about 20 minutes. Cut into 20 to 24 pieces.

★ **YIELD: 20–24 PIECES**

BARS

Crisp Rice Treats

I used to make Rice Crispy treats all the time when I was in seventh grade. Today my kids eat them. I even take a bite from time to time. You can mix in whatever you want. I like to halve the recipe and cut out shapes with cookie cutters. I once even went so far as to pick out the red pieces for Valentine's Day and cut the "cookies" with heart-shaped cookie cutters.

2 tablespoons unsalted butter

1 package (10 ounces) mini marshmallows, about 4 cups

6 cups crisp rice cereal (multicolored is prettiest)

1 to 2 cups semisweet or milk chocolate or peanut butter chips, mini M&Ms, or Heath Bar chips

Lightly grease a 9 x 13-inch pan and, if desired, line with parchment paper. Lightly grease a spatula.

Place the butter in a skillet over low heat, and when it has melted, add the marshmallows and cook until melted. Add the crisp rice cereal and the chips or other optional ingredients, if using, and quickly mix with the spatula. Transfer to the pan and pat down. Set aside and when cool cut into 24 bars.

★ YIELD: 24 BARS

The Late Jake and Earl's Seven-Layer Bars

Although these bars are classic Americana, I first tasted them at the now-defunct Jake and Earl's BBQ in Cambridge, Massachusetts. I will forever think of them as an invention of owners Cary Wheaton and Chris Schlesinger.

¼ cup (4 tablespoons) unsalted butter, melted

1 sleeve graham crackers, crumbled (do not use low fat)

½ cup unsweetened or sweetened shredded coconut, or a combination, plus additional for garnish

1 cup semisweet chocolate chips

1 cup butterscotch chips

¾ cup sweetened condensed milk

1 cup pecans, coarsely chopped

BARS

Preheat the oven to 350 degrees.

Place the butter and graham crackers in a bowl and combine well. Press into an 8-inch-square pan. Sprinkle the coconut evenly over the crust. Sprinkle the chocolate morsels evenly over the coconut layer. Sprinkle the butterscotch chips over the chocolate chips. Pour the condensed milk evenly over the chocolate layer. Sprinkle the pecans evenly over the condensed milk layer. Press the layers down, transfer to the oven, and bake for about 30 minutes.

Cut into 16 pieces and garnish with additional coconut, if desired.

★ **YIELD: 16 BARS**

Apple Cranberry Oatmeal Bars

These almost effortless bars say "autumn." Of course, if you play around with the filling and use peaches, pears, or berries, they will evoke an entirely different season. The components can be assembled several hours or even days ahead of time for an even quicker dessert.

For the filling:
3 Granny Smith apples, peeled, cored, and chopped or thinly sliced
2½ to 3 cups cranberries (1 bag)
½ cup sugar

For the crust:
2½ cups rolled oats
2 cups all-purpose flour
1¼ cups light brown sugar
2 teaspoons ground cinnamon
1 teaspoon baking soda
1 teaspoon kosher salt
½ pound (2 sticks) unsalted butter, melted

Preheat the oven to 350 degrees. Lightly grease a 9 x 13-inch pan

To make the filling: Place the apples, cranberries, and sugar in a saucepan and bring to a low boil over medium heat. Lower the heat to low and cook, stirring occasionally, until soft and syrupy, about 15 to 20 minutes. Set aside to cool.

To make the crust: Place the oats, flour, sugar, cinnamon, baking soda, and salt in a bowl and mix to combine. Add the butter and mix well. Remove ⅔ of the crust mixture and pat down into the prepared pan. Pour the cooled fruit over the crust and top with the remaining crust mixture. Pat down and transfer to the oven. Bake until lightly browned, about 45 minutes. Cool and cut into 20 to 24 pieces.

Variation:

FOR CRANBERRY ONLY BARS: INCREASE THE CRANBERRIES TO 5 TO 6 CUPS, OMIT THE APPLES, AND INCREASE THE SUGAR TO 1½ CUPS.

★ **YIELD: 20–24 BARS**

Breakfast, Pound, and Tea Cakes, Cupcakes, and Baby Cakes

All of the cake and bread recipes that follow can also be made into muffins, mini bundts, mini loaves, or whatever small pan you like to use.

TO TRANSPORT AND DISPLAY CAKES

Line a box that is at least 2 inches deeper than the cake with a clean dish towel. Place the cake on a plate, lower to the bottom of the box, and, if necessary, secure by placing toothpicks on the sides of the cake, which will prevent the sides of the cake from touching the sides of the box.

Be sure to cut slices; no one will want to ask you to cut it open. Wrap slices and cupcakes with plastic wrap, if desired.

Buttery Pound Cake

Your basic pound cake: buttery, moist, simple, and rich.

This versatile cake can be made into one 10-inch bundt, two 9 x 5-inch loaf cakes, one 9 x 5-inch and two 8 x 4-inch loaf cakes, or four 8 x 4-inch loaf cakes.

1 pound (4 sticks) unsalted butter, at room temperature

3 cups sugar

6 eggs, at room temperature

4 cups all-purpose flour

1 cup whole or 2% milk

1 tablespoon vanilla extract

2 teaspoons baking powder

½ teaspoon kosher salt

BREAKFAST, POUND, AND TEA CAKES, CUPCAKES, AND BABY CAKES

Preheat the oven to 350 degrees. Generously grease and flour the pan(s).

Place the butter and sugar in the bowl of a mixer fitted with a paddle and beat until smooth and creamy. Add the eggs, one at a time, beating well and scraping down the bowl before each addition. Add 2 cups of the flour and beat well. Scrape down the sides of the bowl and add the milk and vanilla, continuing to beat.

Scrape down the sides of the bowl and add the baking powder, salt, and the remaining 2 cups of flour. Beat well.

Pour the batter into the prepared pan(s). If you are using more than one pan, be sure the batter comes to the halfway point. Transfer to the oven and bake until the cake pulls away from the sides of the pan and a tester comes out clean, about 1 hour for the bundt pan, 50 minutes for the 9 x 5-inch loaf pan, and 45 minutes for the smaller pans.

Cool for 20 minutes in the pan and then invert on a rack. Cool to room temperature and cut into 12 to 16 pieces.

Sydny Miner's Mexican Chocolate Pound Cake

The addition of cocoa and cinnamon makes this pound cake anything but basic. But be forewarned: The cocoa makes an overbaked cake dry, so be very careful not to overcook it.

If you don't want to warm the milk to room temperature or cool the coffee to room temperature, simply add the cold milk to the hot coffee and then add the mixture to the batter.

This cake can be made into one 10-inch bundt, two 9 x 5-inch loaf cakes, one 9 x 5-inch and two 8 x 4-inch loaf cakes, or four 8 x 4-inch loaf cakes.

BREAKFAST, POUND, AND TEA CAKES, CUPCAKES, AND BABY CAKES

3½ cups all-purpose flour

1 cup unsweetened cocoa powder

2 teaspoons ground cinnamon

2 teaspoons baking powder

½ teaspoon kosher salt

1 pound (4 sticks) unsalted butter, at room temperature

2 cups light brown sugar, firmly packed

1 cup sugar

6 eggs, at room temperature

½ cup whole or 2% milk, at room temperature

½ cup strong coffee, at room temperature

1 tablespoon vanilla extract

Preheat the oven to 350 degrees. Generously grease and flour the pan(s).

Sift the flour, cocoa powder, cinnamon, baking powder, and salt into a bowl.

Place the butter and sugars in the bowl of a mixer fitted with a paddle and beat until smooth and creamy. Add the eggs, one at a time, beating well and scraping down the sides of the bowl before each addition. Add half the flour mixture and beat well. Scrape down the sides of the bowl and add the milk, coffee, and vanilla, continuing to beat.

Scrape down the sides of the bowl, add the remaining half of the flour mixture, and beat well.

Pour the batter into the prepared pan(s). If you are using more than one pan, be sure the batter comes to the halfway point. Transfer to the oven and bake until the cake pulls away from the sides of the pan and a tester comes out not quite clean, with just a bit of crumb, about 50 to 55 minutes for the bundt pan, 45 minutes for the 9 x 5-inch loaf pan, and 40 minutes for the smaller pans.

Cool for 20 minutes in the pan and then invert on a rack. Cool to room temperature.

Jill Weber's Apricot Brandy Sour Cream Pound Cake

Jill Weber, my friend and the designer of this book, gave me this recipe that she's been making for thirty years. It's basically a classic pound cake with an apricot kick.

1 cup coarsely chopped dried apricots

½ cup apricot brandy, Cointreau, Grand Marnier, Triple Sec, or Amaretto

¾ cup apricot nectar or orange juice

1 teaspoon grated or finely chopped orange zest

2 cups sugar

½ pound (2 sticks) unsalted butter, at room temperature

6 eggs, at room temperature

1 tablespoon vanilla extract

3 cups all-purpose flour

1 cup sour cream

2 teaspoons baking powder

1 teaspoon kosher salt

½ teaspoon baking soda

Place the apricots, brandy, and apricot nectar in a small saucepan and bring to a low boil over medium heat. Off heat, cover and set aside for at least 20 minutes.

Preheat the oven to 325 degrees. Lightly grease a tube or bundt pan.

Place the orange zest and sugar in the bowl of a mixer fitted with a paddle and spin/mix for 5 minutes. Add the butter and beat until light and fluffy. Add the eggs, one at a time, beating well and scraping down the sides of the bowl before each addition. Add the vanilla and mix.

Add 1½ cups of the flour and beat well. Scrape down the sides of the bowl and add ½ cup of the sour cream.

Scrape down the sides of the bowl, add the remaining 1½ cups flour, baking powder, salt, and baking soda, and beat well.

Scrape down the sides of the bowl and add the remaining ½ cup sour cream.

Drain the apricots and set aside the extra liquid. Fold the apricots into the batter, scrape down the sides of the bowl, and gently spoon the batter into the prepared pan. Transfer to the oven and bake until a tester comes out clean, about 1 hour. Cool for 5 minutes and prick the surface of the cake with a toothpick. Brush on the reserved liquid and cool to room temperature.

Cardamom Coffee Cake

Rich, buttery, and aromatic, this is an old standby for me.

For the filling:

1 cup toasted chopped walnuts (see note on page 28)

½ cup sugar

1 tablespoon ground cinnamon

For the cake:

½ pound (2 sticks) unsalted butter, at room temperature

2 cups sugar

2 eggs, at room temperature

2 cups all-purpose flour

2 cups sour cream or whole milk plain yogurt

1 tablespoon ground cardamom

1 tablespoon baking powder

¼ teaspoon kosher salt

1 teaspoon vanilla extract

Preheat the oven to 350 degrees. Generously grease and flour a bundt pan.

To make the filling: Place the walnuts, sugar, and cinnamon in a small mixing bowl, mix well, and set aside.

To make the cake: Place the butter and sugar in the bowl of a mixer fitted with a paddle and beat until light, fluffy, and light lemon colored, about 3 to 5 minutes. Add the eggs, one at a time, beating well and scraping down the sides of the bowl before each addition. Add 1 cup of the flour and beat well. Scrape down the sides of the bowl and add 1 cup of the sour cream, continuing to beat.

Scrape down the sides of the bowl, add the cardamom, baking powder, salt, and the remaining 1 cup flour, and beat well. Add the remaining 1 cup sour cream and the vanilla and beat well.

Scrape down the sides of the bowl and pour one-third of the batter into the prepared pan. Sprinkle with half of the filling mixture. Repeat and then top with the remaining one-third batter. Transfer to the oven and bake until the cake pulls away from the sides of the pan and a tester comes out clean, about 1 hour.

Cool for 20 minutes in the pan and then invert on a rack. Cool to room temperature.

Sour Cream Poppy Seed Cake

This is probably my favorite cake in this book; it is not simply a pound cake with poppy seeds, though it is, in fact, basically a pound cake with poppy seeds in it. It is so, so, so, so much better. If you love poppy seeds, you must try this cake. However, you must be a poppy seed lover with inner strength: it is best to make it 2 to 3 days ahead of time and let it sit well wrapped. It can also be iced with Cream Cheese Icing (page 183).

1 cup whole milk

¾ cup poppy seeds

½ cup sour cream or whole milk plain yogurt

1 tablespoon vanilla extract

2 tablespoons fresh lemon juice

½ pound (2 sticks) unsalted butter, at room temperature

1⅓ cups sugar

3 eggs, at room temperature

2 cups all-purpose flour

1 tablespoon baking powder

½ teaspoon kosher salt

Preheat the oven to 350 degrees. Lightly grease a bundt pan.

Place the milk and poppy seeds in a small saucepan and bring to a low boil over medium-high heat. Set aside to cool for 15 minutes. Add the sour cream, vanilla, and lemon juice and mix well.

Place the butter and sugar in the bowl of a mixer fitted with a paddle and beat until light, fluffy, and a pale lemon color, about 3 to 5 minutes. Add the eggs, one at a time, beating well and scraping down the sides of the bowl before each addition. Add 1 cup of the flour and beat well. Scrape down the sides of the bowl and add half of the reserved poppy seed mixture, continuing to beat.

Scrape down the sides of the bowl, add the baking powder, salt, and the remaining 1 cup flour, and beat well. Scrape down the sides of the bowl, add the remaining half of the poppy seed mixture, and mix well. Scrape down the sides of the bowl and pour into the prepared pan. Transfer to the oven and bake until the top is just golden and a knife inserted comes out clean, about 45 to 50 minutes.

Citrus Poppy Seed Cake

My second favorite cake in this book, this cake gets its kick from citrus and its crunch from poppy seeds.

For the cake:

1 cup whole milk

¾ cup poppy seeds

½ cup sour cream or whole milk plain yogurt

1 tablespoon vanilla extract

½ cup plus 2 tablespoons fresh lemon juice

Grated zest of 5 lemons or 6 oranges

1⅓ cups sugar

½ pound (2 sticks) unsalted butter, at room temperature

3 eggs, at room temperature

2 cups all-purpose flour

1 tablespoon baking powder

½ teaspoon kosher salt

For the lemon syrup:

½ cup fresh lemon juice

½ cup confectioners' sugar

or

For the orange syrup:

2 tablespoons fresh lemon juice

6 tablespoons fresh orange juice

⅓ cup confectioners' sugar

Preheat the oven to 350 degrees. Lightly grease a bundt pan.

To make the cake: Place the milk and poppy seeds in a small saucepan and bring to a low boil over medium-high heat. Set aside to cool for 15 minutes. Add the sour cream, vanilla, and lemon juice and mix well.

Place the lemon zest and sugar in the bowl of a mixer fitted with a paddle and let spin for 5 minutes. Add the butter and beat until light, fluffy, and light lemon colored, about 3 to 5 minutes. Add the eggs, one at a time, beating well and scraping down the sides of the bowl before each addition.

Add 1 cup of the flour and beat well. Scrape down the sides of the bowl and add half of the reserved poppy seed mixture, continuing to beat.

Scrape down the sides of the bowl, add the baking powder, salt, and the remaining 1 cup flour, and beat well. Scrape down the sides of the bowl, add the remaining half of the poppy seed mixture, and mix well. Scrape down the sides of the bowl and place in the prepared pan. Transfer to the oven and bake until the top is just golden and a knife inserted comes out clean, about 45 to 50 minutes.

To make the syrup: Place the lemon or lemon and orange juices and sugar in a saucepan and bring to a boil over high heat. Set aside to cool to room temperature and then brush on the warm cake.

BREAKFAST, POUND, AND TEA CAKES, CUPCAKES, AND BABY CAKES

Frajil Farms Deceptive Yogurt Cake

The tang of the yogurt makes Jill Weber's light poundlike cake taste as if it has much more lemon in it than it actually does. The yogurt also gives the impression that it is low in fat. However, when you look at the butter content of this cake, you realize that the yogurt was put in for its taste rather than for its low calorie count.

For the cake:
½ pound (2 sticks) unsalted butter, at room temperature
1½ cups sugar
1 teaspoon vanilla extract
3 eggs, at room temperature
2¼ cups all-purpose flour
½ teaspoon kosher salt
½ teaspoon baking soda
1 cup plain low-fat or whole milk yogurt
1 tablespoon grated lemon zest

For the icing:
1 cup confectioners' sugar
3 tablespoons fresh lemon juice
Grated zest of 1 lemon

Preheat the oven to 375 degrees. Grease a tube or bundt pan.

Place the butter and sugar in the bowl of a mixer fitted with a paddle and beat until light, fluffy, and light lemon colored, about 3 to 5 minutes. Add the vanilla and eggs, one at a time, beating well and scraping down the sides of the bowl before each addition.

Scrape down the sides of the bowl, add the flour, salt, and baking soda, and beat well. Add the yogurt and lemon zest and beat well. Scrape down the sides of the bowl and pour into the prepared pan. Transfer to the oven and bake until the top is a light golden brown, about 55 minutes. Cool for 20 minutes in the pan and then invert onto a rack.

To make the icing: Place the sugar, lemon juice, and lemon zest in a bowl and mix until smooth and creamy. When the cake has cooled completely, spread with the icing. Cut into 12 to 16 slices.

Walnut Rum Spice Cake

Not for teetotalers; you can definitely taste the rum in this dense, nutty cake.

For the cake:

½ pound (2 sticks) unsalted butter, at room temperature

1½ cups dark brown sugar

2 eggs, at room temperature

1 teaspoon vanilla extract

2 cups all-purpose flour

1 teaspoon baking soda

1 teaspoon ground cinnamon

1 teaspoon ground nutmeg

1 teaspoon ground cardamom

½ teaspoon kosher salt

½ cup buttermilk or plain yogurt

1½ cups finely chopped toasted walnuts or pecans (see note on page 28)

For the soaking syrup:

1 cup sugar

1 cup rum

¼ cup (4 tablespoons) unsalted butter

Preheat the oven to 350 degrees. Lightly grease a bundt pan.

To make the cake: Place the butter and sugar in a mixer fitted with a paddle and beat until light, fluffy, and a light caramel color, about 3 to 5 minutes. Add the eggs, one at a time, beating well and scraping down the sides of the bowl before each addition. Scrape down the sides of the bowl and add the vanilla.

Place the flour, baking soda, cinnamon, nutmeg, cardamom, and salt in a mixing bowl and mix to combine.

Add one-third of the dry ingredients to the butter and egg mixture and beat well. Scrape down the sides of the bowl and add half of the buttermilk, continuing to beat. Repeat and then add the remaining one-third of the dry ingredients, beating well. Add the walnuts. Scrape down the sides of the bowl and pour the batter into the prepared pan. Transfer to the oven and bake until lightly golden and springy on top and until the cake just pulls away from the sides of the pan, about 40 minutes to 1 hour.

To make the soaking syrup: Place the sugar, rum, and butter in a small saucepan and bring to a boil over medium heat. Set aside.

Cool the cake in the pan for 10 minutes, and, while the cake is still in the pan, pour the soaking syrup over it. When fully cooled, cover with plastic wrap and store at room temperature for 2 days. Cut into 12 to 14 slices.

Prune Sour Cream Coffee Cake

A wonderful, dense coffee cake that could get its flavor from any variety of dried fruits, including dried cranberries, cherries, dates, or apricots. I'd pass on raisins, though.

1 cup pitted prunes, chopped

½ cup boiling water

1 teaspoon grated lemon zest

½ cup brown sugar

½ cup chopped toasted walnuts (see note on page 28)

1½ teaspoons ground cinnamon

2 cups all-purpose flour

1 teaspoon baking soda

1 teaspoon baking powder

½ teaspoon kosher salt

½ pound (2 sticks) unsalted butter, at room temperature

1 cup sugar

2 eggs, at room temperature

1 cup sour cream

1 teaspoon vanilla extract

Preheat the oven to 350 degrees. Lightly butter a 9-inch tube or bundt pan.

Place the prunes and boiling water in a small bowl and set aside for 30 minutes. Drain, discarding the liquid, and add the lemon zest to the prunes. Set aside.

Place the brown sugar, walnuts, and cinnamon in a bowl and set aside.

Place the flour, baking soda, baking powder, and salt in a bowl and mix to combine.

Place the butter and sugar in the bowl of a mixer fitted with a paddle and beat until light, fluffy, and light lemon colored, about 3 to 5 minutes. Add the eggs, one at a time, beating well and scraping down the sides of the bowl before each addition. Scrape down the sides of the bowl, add one-third of the flour mixture, and beat well. Add half of the sour cream and the vanilla. Repeat and add the remaining third of the flour mixture and mix well. Add the reserved prunes and mix until just combined.

Scrape down the sides of the bowl and pour one-third of the batter into the prepared pan. Sprinkle with half of the filling mixture. Repeat and then top with the remaining third of the batter. Transfer to the oven and bake until the cake pulls away from the sides of the pan and a tester comes out clean, about 45 to 55 minutes. Cool the cake in the pan for 10 minutes and then invert onto a rack.

Cut into 12 to 16 pieces.

Cranberry Walnut Coffee Cake

I just had to include this cake, which has been altered from the original recipe in Sarah Leah Chase's *The Open House Nantucket Cookbook*. I've probably made it for more brunches than seems possible. In fact, I make it so often, I buy a long-lasting supply of cranberries in the fall so that when I want to make it in the spring, I have a supply in the freezer.

You can substitute blueberries, raspberries, or pitted cherries for the cranberries or entirely omit them for a more basic coffee cake.

For the cake:
¼ pound (1 stick) unsalted butter, at room temperature

1 cup sugar

2 eggs, at room temperature

1 teaspoon vanilla extract

1 tablespoon grated orange zest

2 cups all-purpose flour

1 teaspoon baking soda

1 teaspoon baking powder

½ teaspoon kosher salt

1 cup sour cream

2½ cups cranberries

For the topping:
¾ cup brown sugar

½ cup all-purpose flour

2 teaspoons ground cinnamon

¼ cup (4 tablespoons) unsalted butter

½ cup coarsely chopped walnuts

Preheat the oven to 350 degrees. Butter and lightly flour a 13 x 9-inch pan.

Place the butter and sugar in the bowl of a mixer fitted with a paddle and beat until light, fluffy, and light lemon colored, about 3 to 5 minutes. Add the eggs, one at a time, beating well and scraping down the sides of the bowl before each addition. Add the vanilla and orange zest and beat well. Add the flour, baking soda, baking powder, and salt and mix well. Add the sour cream and mix until smooth. Spoon into the prepared pan and top with the cranberries.

To make the topping: Place the sugar, flour, and cinnamon in a small mixing bowl and toss to combine. Add the butter, in pieces, and mix until crumbly. Add the walnuts and sprinkle the topping over the cranberries. Transfer to the oven and bake until a cake tester inserted in the center comes out clean, about 45 minutes. Cut into 24 pieces and serve warm or at room temperature.

BREAKFAST, POUND, AND TEA CAKES, CUPCAKES, AND BABY CAKES

Banana Streusel Coffee Cake

Although I like almost nothing better than Paige's Astounding Banana Bread (page 188) and/or a fruit smoothie, sometimes I want to make something different with a funky banana. This wonderful light-flavored banana coffee cake is more like a coffee cake and less like banana bread.

For the topping:

¼ cup (4 tablespoons) unsalted butter, chilled or at room temperature

⅓ cup sugar

⅓ cup all-purpose flour

⅓ to ½ cup chopped toasted walnuts (optional) (see note on page 28)

For the cake:

¼ cup (4 tablespoons) unsalted butter, at room temperature

6 tablespoons sugar

1 teaspoon vanilla extract

2 eggs, at room temperature

2 overripe bananas, mashed

1 cup plus 6 tablespoons all-purpose flour

1½ teaspoons baking powder

½ teaspoon baking soda

½ teaspoon kosher salt

½ teaspoon ground cinnamon

⅓ cup plain yogurt, buttermilk, or sour cream

Preheat the oven to 375 degrees. Lightly grease an 8 x 8-inch pan.

To make the topping: Place the butter, sugar, and flour in a mixer fitted with a paddle or food processor fitted with a steel blade and mix until combined and crumbly. Add the walnuts, if using, mix to combine, and set aside.

To make the cake: Place the butter, sugar, and vanilla in the bowl of a mixer fitted with a paddle and beat until light, fluffy, and light lemon colored, about 3 to 5 minutes. Add the eggs, one at a time, beating well and scraping down before each addition. Add the bananas and mix until well combined. Scrape down the sides of the bowl and add the flour, baking powder, baking soda, salt, and cinnamon, and mix until well combined. Add the yogurt and mix until smooth. Scrape down the sides of the bowl and pour into the prepared pan.

Cover with the reserved topping and transfer to the oven. Bake until the top is just beginning to lightly brown, about 30 to 35 minutes. Cut into 9 wedges.

BREAKFAST, POUND, AND TEA CAKES, CUPCAKES, AND BABY CAKES

Dessert, Bundt, and Layer Cakes

When I owned From the Night Kitchen, I hated making whole cakes for special orders because, unlike bars and cookies, I couldn't sample them to be sure they were okay. I still have some residual hesitation, but experience has given me confidence.

Of course, cakes do require a little more exactitude: if you can, have all your ingredients at room temperature. If you can't, don't worry.

TO TRANSPORT AND DISPLAY CAKES

Line a box that is at least 2 inches deeper than the cake with a clean dish towel. Place the cake on a plate, lower to the bottom of the box, and, if necessary, secure by placing toothpicks on the sides of the cake, which will prevent the sides of the cake from touching the sides of the box.

If you are travelling a long distance, you may want to ice your cake at the bake sale. Be sure to cut slices; no one will want to ask you to cut it open. Wrap slices with plastic wrap, if desired.

Buttermilk-Glazed Apple Cake Studded with Coconut and Walnuts

This is the cake that inspired this book. It never misses.

For the cake:

1½ cups sugar

1¼ cups canola or corn oil

3 eggs, at room temperature

¼ cup apple or orange juice

1 teaspoon vanilla extract

3 cups all-purpose flour

1 teaspoon baking soda

1 teaspoon ground cinnamon

¼ teaspoon kosher salt

2 Granny Smith apples, peeled, cored, and finely chopped

½ cup shredded sweetened or unsweetened coconut, or a combination (optional)

½ cup chopped toasted walnuts (optional) (see note on page 28)

For the soaking syrup:

½ cup buttermilk

¼ cup sugar

2 tablespoons unsalted butter

½ teaspoon baking soda

Preheat the oven to 325 degrees. Lightly grease and flour a 10-inch bundt or tube pan.

Place the sugar, oil, eggs, juice, vanilla, flour, baking soda, cinnamon, and salt in the bowl of a mixer fitted with a paddle and beat until just combined.

Scrape down the sides of the bowl and add, by hand, the apples and the coconut, if using, and walnuts, if using. Mix until combined. Place in the prepared pan, transfer to the oven, and bake until a tester comes out clean, about 50 to 60 minutes. Cool the cake in the pan for 15 minutes and then invert onto a rack.

To make the soaking syrup: Place the buttermilk, sugar, butter, and baking soda in a small saucepan and bring to a boil over high heat.

Cool the cake in the pan for 5 minutes and prick the surface of the cake with a toothpick. Brush on the soaking syrup and cool to room temperature. Invert and remove cake. Cut into 14 to 16 pieces.

Banana Cake

This is the cake I made for both my children's first birthdays when I didn't feel they were quite ready for chocolate or I for the mess and bellyaches I was anticipating.

The cake can be served bare or iced with Dark Chocolate Ganache (page 180), Caramel Icing (page 182), Cream Cheese Icing (page 183), or Seven-Minute Icing (page 184).

2 cups sugar

1 cup canola or vegetable oil

3 eggs, room temperature

1 tablespoon vanilla extract

4 overripe bananas, mashed with a fork

3 cups all-purpose flour

1 teaspoon baking soda

1 teaspoon kosher salt

½ teaspoon baking powder

½ teaspoon ground cinnamon

½ teaspoon ground nutmeg

Preheat the oven to 325 degrees. Lightly grease a bundt pan.

Place the sugar, oil, and eggs in the bowl of a mixer fitted with a paddle and mix until light and lemon colored. Add the vanilla and bananas and mix until just combined. Scrape down the sides of the bowl, add the flour, baking soda, salt, baking powder, cinnamon, and nutmeg, and mix until just combined. Scrape down the sides of the bowl and pour into the prepared bundt pan. Transfer to the oven and bake until a toothpick comes out clean, about 1 hour.

Cool the cake in the pan for 20 minutes and then invert onto a rack. Cool to room temperature. Cut into 12 to 16 pieces.

Verdi's Double Lemon Cake
with Fresh Lemon Zest Glaze

Mark's college roommate, John Verderesee, whom we call Verdi, loves lemon cake; whenever there's something for him to celebrate, I make this cake. Over the years, I have added more and more lemon, and now, after adding still more, I am finally done. If you're using flavored yogurt, I suggest you use Stonyfield. Don't use a custard-style or gelatin-stabilized variety.

For a fancier presentation, bake the cake in two layer pans and spread purchased or, if you are determined, fresh lemon curd between the layers. Cover the whole thing with Seven-Minute Icing (page 184) and then with shredded coconut.

For the cake:

½ pound (2 sticks) unsalted butter, at room temperature

2 cups sugar (use 1¾ cups if using lemon yogurt)

3 eggs, at room temperature

3 cups all-purpose flour

1 cup buttermilk or plain or lemon yogurt

½ teaspoon baking soda

½ teaspoon kosher salt

2 tablespoons grated lemon zest

2 tablespoons fresh lemon juice

For the glaze:

½ cup confectioners' sugar (or for an icing, increase to 1 cup)

½ cup lemon juice

3 tablespoons grated lemon zest

Preheat the oven to 350 degrees. Grease a bundt pan.

Place the butter and sugar in the bowl of a mixer fitted with a paddle and beat until light, fluffy, and light lemon colored, about 3 to 5 minutes. Add the eggs, one at a time, beating well and scraping down the sides of the bowl before each addition. Add 1 cup of the flour and beat well. Scrape down the sides of the bowl and add ½ cup of the buttermilk, continuing to beat. Add 1 cup of the flour, baking soda, and salt and beat well. Scrape down the sides of the bowl and add the remaining ½ cup buttermilk, lemon zest, and lemon juice, continuing to beat. Add the remaining 1 cup flour and beat well.

Scrape down the sides of the bowl and spoon into the prepared pan. Transfer to the oven and bake until light golden, about 45 to 55 minutes.

To make the glaze: Place the sugar, lemon juice, and lemon zest in a small mixing bowl and beat until smooth. Set aside.

Cool the cake in the pan for 10 minutes and then invert onto a rack. Prick the surface with a toothpick. Brush on the glaze and cool to room temperature. If using icing, let the cake cool to room temperature first. Cut into 12 to 16 pieces.

Dain Fritz's Grandmother's Carrot Cake

There's not an occasion I haven't made this cake for: a wedding, baby showers, birthday parties, dinner parties. I've had this recipe for twenty-five years and after trying many other carrot cakes, I still feel it's the best one ever.

Although this cake is great alone, it's best smothered with Cream Cheese Icing (page 183).

3 cups grated carrots

2 cups sugar

1 cup vegetable or canola oil

4 eggs, at room temperature

2 cups all-purpose flour

2 teaspoons baking soda

1 teaspoon kosher salt

1 teaspoon ground cinnamon

Whole or chopped walnuts, for garnish

Preheat the oven to 350 degrees. Lightly grease and flour a 10-inch bundt or ring pan, an 8 x 13-inch baking pan, or two 9-inch cake pans.

Place the carrots, sugar, oil, and eggs in the bowl of a mixer fitted with a paddle and beat until combined. Add the flour, baking soda, salt, and cinnamon and beat until combined.

Scrape down the sides of the bowl and place in the prepared pan. Transfer to the oven and bake until a tester comes out clean,

DESSERT, BUNDT, AND LAYER CAKES

about 40 minutes for the bundt and 8 x 13-inch pan or 25 minutes for the cake pans. Cool the cake(s) in the pan for 15 minutes and then, if using the bundt or cake pans, invert onto a rack. Cool to room temperature.

While the cake is baking, prepare the Cream Cheese Icing (page 183). When the cake has cooled completely, spread with the icing. Garnish with chopped nuts, if using. Cut into 14 pieces.

Rum-Spiked Pumpkin and Nut Cake

This recipe was part of Bercie's collection (my biggest source of recipes). It surprised me because I couldn't imagine what the end result would taste like. It was great.

If you have a small amount of pumpkin puree left, you can add it to the icing.

For the cake:

1½ cups plus 2 tablespoons all-purpose flour

½ to ¾ cup chopped toasted pecans (see note on page 28)

½ teaspoon baking soda

½ teaspoon baking powder

½ teaspoon kosher salt

½ cup plain low-fat yogurt

¾ cup canned pumpkin puree, at room temperature

¼ to ½ cup rum, to taste

1 teaspoon vanilla extract

6 tablespoons unsalted butter, at room temperature

¾ cup sugar

2 eggs, at room temperature

For the icing:

1 cup confectioners' sugar

2 tablespoons orange juice

Preheat the oven to 350 degrees. Lightly grease an 8 x 8-inch pan or a 9-inch cake pan.

Place the flour, pecans, baking soda, baking powder, and salt in a mixing bowl and mix to combine.

Place the yogurt, pumpkin, rum, and vanilla in a bowl and mix.

Place the butter and sugar in the bowl of a mixer fitted with a paddle and mix until light, fluffy, and light lemon colored, about 3 to 5 minutes. Add the eggs, one at a time, beating well and scraping down the sides of the bowl before each addition. Scrape down the sides of the bowl, add one-third of the flour mixture, and mix until just combined. Scrape down the sides of the bowl, add half the yogurt mixture, and mix until just combined. Repeat with the second third of the flour and the remaining yogurt.

Add the remaining third of the flour mixture and mix. Scrape down the sides of the bowl and spoon into the prepared pan.

Transfer to the oven and bake until lightly golden and springy on top and until the cake pulls away from the sides of the pan, about 25 to 30 minutes. Set aside to cool.

To make the icing: Place the sugar in a bowl and slowly add the orange juice, stirring constantly.

Spread the icing over the cake and cut into 9 to 12 pieces.

Classic Butter Cake

The perfect cake for dressing up. I think it's particularly delicious served with Dark Chocolate Ganache (page 180) or Milk Chocolate Ganache (page181).

Using sour cream will give this cake the longest life, buttermilk the shortest.

3 cups cake flour

1 tablespoon baking powder

¼ teaspoon kosher salt

1 cup milk, buttermilk, sour cream, or plain yogurt, at room temperature

2 teaspoons vanilla extract

½ pound (2 sticks) unsalted butter, at room temperature

2 cups sugar

3 eggs, at room temperature

2 egg yolks, at room temperature

Preheat the oven to 350 degrees. Lightly grease and flour two 9-inch layer pans.

Place the flour, baking powder, and salt in a bowl and mix to combine.

Place the milk and vanilla in a bowl and mix to combine.

Place the butter and sugar in the bowl of a mixer fitted with a paddle and beat until light, fluffy, and pale lemon colored, about 3 to 5 minutes. Add the eggs and egg yolks, one at a time, beating well and scraping down the sides of the bowl before each addition.

Scrape down the sides of the bowl, add one-third of the flour mixture, and beat well. Scrape down the sides of the bowl, add half the milk mixture, and beat well. Repeat with the second third of the flour and the remaining milk. Add the remaining third of the flour mixture and beat well. Scrape down the sides of the bowl and spoon into the prepared pans.

Transfer to the oven and bake until lightly golden and springy on top, about 35 minutes. Cool in the pan for 10 minutes, then invert on a rack to cool completely. If you want a four-layer cake, carefully split each layer through the center.

While the cake is baking, make the ganache or icing of your choice. When the cake has cooled completely, ice each layer, assemble, and then ice the sides. Cut into 12 to 14 pieces.

White Chocolate Cake

A wonderful cake when you want something simple but don't want the Classic Butter Cake (page 159). The white chocolate adds a buttery, rather than a chocolatey flavor. Although the pecans and coconut are optional, their addition makes this cake exceptional.

Callebaut and Lindt white chocolate are especially good here, and both are available at most grocery or specialty markets.

Serve with Dark Chocolate Ganache (page 180) or Milk Chocolate Ganache (page 181).

½ pound (2 sticks) unsalted butter, at room temperature

2 cups sugar

¼ pound Callebaut or Lindt white chocolate, gently melted over a double boiler and cooled

4 eggs, at room temperature

2½ cups cake flour

¼ teaspoon baking powder

¼ teaspoon kosher salt

1 cup buttermilk

1 teaspoon vanilla extract

1 cup chopped toasted pecans (optional) (see note on page 28)

1 cup unsweetened or sweetened shredded coconut (optional)

Preheat the oven to 350 degrees. Lightly grease and flour two 9-inch cake pans or 24 cupcake tins.

Place the butter and sugar in the bowl of a mixer fitted with a paddle and mix until light, fluffy, and pale lemon colored, about 3 to 5 minutes. Add the melted chocolate and mix until well combined. Add the eggs, one at a time, beating well and scraping down the sides of the bowl before each addition.

Place the flour, baking powder, and salt in a bowl and mix to combine.

Place the buttermilk and vanilla in a bowl and mix to combine.

Scrape down the sides of the bowl, add one-third of the flour mixture, and beat well. Scrape down the sides of the bowl, add half the milk mixture, and beat well. Repeat with the second third of the flour and the remaining milk. Add the remaining third of the flour mixture. Gently fold in the pecans and/or coconut, if using. Scrape down the sides of the bowl and spoon into the prepared pans.

Transfer to the oven and bake until lightly golden and springy on top, about 35 minutes. Invert the cake onto a rack and set aside to cool. For a four-layer cake, split each layer through the center.

While the cake is cooling, make the ganache. When the cake has cooled completely, ice each layer and the sides. Cut into 12 to 14 pieces.

New England Maple Cake
with Maple Frosting

A light but rich cake that deserves the finest, darkest *real* maple syrup you can find.

For the cake:

2 cups all-purpose flour

1 tablespoon baking powder

¾ teaspoon kosher salt

1 cup maple syrup

1 cup heavy cream

2 eggs, at room temperature, lightly beaten

¼ pound (1 stick) unsalted butter, melted

For the frosting:

¼ cup (4 tablespoons) unsalted butter, at room temperature

2 cups confectioners' sugar

⅓ cup maple syrup

Walnut halves or chopped walnuts, for garnish (optional)

Preheat the oven to 350 degrees. Butter a 9 x 13-inch pan and line the bottom with waxed paper or parchment paper.

To make the cake: Place the flour, baking powder, and salt in the bowl of a mixer fitted with a paddle and mix to combine. Add the syrup, cream, and eggs, beating *really* well and scraping down the sides of the bowl before each addition. Add the butter and beat well. Scrape down the sides of the bowl, spoon into the prepared pan, and bake for 35 to 40 minutes, or until a tester comes out clean. Cool the cake in the pan for 5 minutes and then invert onto a rack.

To make the frosting: Place the butter and sugar in the bowl of a mixer fitted with a paddle and beat until light and fluffy. Add the syrup and beat until creamy. Set aside.

When the cake has cooled completely, peel off the paper and carefully flip the cake onto a serving platter. Frost the cake and cut into 24 pieces. Place a walnut half on each piece or sprinkle the top of the cake with the chopped walnuts, if using.

Chocolate Babka

While testing the recipes for this book, I often sent the final product to school for my daughter, Lauren, to share with her kindergarten class. When she took Chocolate Babka to school, her teacher, Lynne Tarr, sent home this message:

> *Dear Sally,*
> *My taste buds but not my waistline thank you for that absolutely delicious cake. Had the whole cake been within reach, it would not have lasted long. Could I have the recipe?*

Well, Lynne, here it is.

2 cups plus 1 teaspoon all-purpose flour

¾ cup plus 1 teaspoon unsweetened cocoa powder

1½ teaspoons baking powder

¾ teaspoon baking soda

½ teaspoon plus ¼ teaspoon kosher salt

1 cup well-chopped semisweet or bittersweet chocolate or chocolate chips

1 cup well-chopped toasted walnuts or pecans (see note on page 28)

¼ cup light brown sugar

1 teaspoon ground cinnamon

½ pound (2 sticks) unsalted butter, at room temperature

1½ cups brown sugar

2 tablespoons honey

1 tablespoon vanilla extract

3 eggs, at room temperature

1½ cups sour cream

Preheat the oven to 350 degrees. Lightly grease a bundt pan. Dust with 1 teaspoon flour and 1 teaspoon cocoa powder.

Place the flour, cocoa, baking powder, baking soda, and ½ teaspoon salt in a mixing bowl and mix to combine.

Place the chocolate, walnuts, sugar, cinnamon, and ¼ teaspoon salt in a mixing bowl and mix to combine.

Place the butter and sugar in the bowl of a mixer fitted with a paddle and beat until light, fluffy, and caramel colored, about 3 to 5 minutes. Add the honey, vanilla, and eggs, one at a time, beating well and scraping down the sides of the bowl before each addition. Add half the flour mixture and beat well. Scrape down the sides of the bowl and add half the sour cream. Add the remaining half of the flour mixture and sour cream and beat well. Do not overmix.

Scrape down the sides of the bowl and pour one-third of the batter into the prepared pan. Sprinkle with half the filling mixture. Repeat and then top with the remaining third of the batter. Transfer to the oven and bake until a tester comes out clean, about 50 to 65 minutes. Cool the cake in the pan for 10 minutes and then invert the cake, leaving it in the pan for 20 minutes more. Remove the pan and then cool completely. Cut into 12 to 16 pieces.

Jane P. Wilson's Never-Fail Chocolate Cake with Classic White Icing

Gracie Gallant, one of Lauren's classmates, went home and raved about the Chocolate Babka (page 165) to her mother, Susan, who offered me this recipe (from her maternal grandmother) in return. She makes it for just about every special occasion, and her husband, David, who swoons every time.

In the world of chocolate cakes, there seem to be seconds between being underdone and overcooked, so be sure to start checking this cake at least a few minutes before I say to do so.

This recipe makes great cupcakes.

DESSERT, BUNDT, AND LAYER CAKES

For the cake:

½ pound (2 sticks) unsalted butter, at room temperature

2 cups sugar

2 eggs, at room temperature

1 cup sour milk (1 tablespoon plus 1 teaspoon vinegar added to enough milk to equal 1 cup)

1 cup unsweetened cocoa powder

3 cups all-purpose flour

2 teaspoons baking soda

2 teaspoons vanilla extract

1 cup hot water

Confectioners' sugar for sprinkling (optional)

For the icing:

1 pound confectioners' sugar

¼ pound (1 stick) unsalted butter, at room temperature

1 teaspoon vanilla extract

3 tablespoons milk

Preheat the oven to 375 degrees. Lightly grease two 9-inch cake pans.

To make the cake: Place the butter and sugar in the bowl of a mixer fitted with a paddle and beat until light, fluffy, and pale yellow. Add the eggs, one at a time, beating well and scraping down the sides of the bowl before each addition. Add the milk and mix to combine. Slowly add the cocoa, flour, and baking soda and mix to combine. Add the vanilla and water and mix until incorporated. Spoon into the prepared pans and transfer to the oven. Bake until a tester comes out with a few crumbs on it, about 22 to 28 minutes. Set aside to cool and spread with the icing or sprinkle with confectioners' sugar or sugar.

To make the icing: Place the confectioners' sugar and butter in the bowl of a food processor and process until smooth. Add the vanilla and milk and process until smooth.

Cut into 12 to 14 pieces.

Black Chocolate Cake

I was looking for a rich black chocolate cake that glistened. Here it is. Serve with Dark Chocolate Ganache (page 180) or Caramel Icing (page 182).

¾ cup unsweetened cocoa powder

1 cup boiling water or prepared coffee

2¾ cups all-purpose flour

2 teaspoons baking soda

½ teaspoon baking powder

½ teaspoon kosher salt

½ pound (2 sticks) unsalted butter, at room temperature

1¾ cups dark brown sugar

1 tablespoon vanilla extract

5 eggs, at room temperature

1 egg white, at room temperature

Preheat the oven to 325 degrees. Lightly grease and flour two or three 9-inch cake pans.

Place the cocoa and water in a small mixing bowl and mix until it forms a smooth paste. Set aside to cool.

Place the flour, baking soda, baking powder, and salt in a mixing bowl and mix to combine.

Place the butter and brown sugar in the bowl of a mixer fitted with a paddle and beat until light and fluffy. Add the cocoa paste, vanilla, eggs, and egg white, one at a time, beating well and scrap-

DESSERT, BUNDT, AND LAYER CAKES

ing down the sides of the bowl before each addition. Add the flour mixture and mix until just combined.

Scrape down the sides of the bowl, spoon into the prepared pans, and bake for 30 to 35 minutes, or until a tester comes out clean. Cool the cakes in the pans for 5 minutes and then invert onto a rack.

While the cake is cooling, make the icing; frost the cake when it is completely cooled.

Coconut Cake with Coconut Syrup

When I was a child, my family used to go to a restaurant called Hamburger Heaven which had branches all over Manhattan (or so it seemed to my ten-year-old self). Although I became a vegetarian when I was a teenager, I continued to go, not for their hamburgers, but for their huge pieces of fabulous coconut cake.

I remember that the cake was packed with coconut. This recipe has been modified so many times, each time adding more and more coconut. This cake is wonderful as it is, if a bit more delicate than the coconut cake of my memory. Hard-core coconut aficionados (like myself) should add Seven-Minute Icing (page 184).

Be sure to buy pure coconut milk with no sugar added.

For the cake:

½ pound (2 sticks) unsalted butter, at room temperature

2 cups sugar

3 eggs, at room temperature

2 egg yolks, at room temperature (reserve the whites for the frosting)

3 cups all-purpose flour

1 tablespoon baking powder

¼ teaspoon kosher salt

1 cup canned coconut milk, at room temperature

2 teaspoons vanilla extract

1 cup unsweetened or sweetened shredded coconut, or a combination

DESSERT, BUNDT, AND LAYER CAKES

For the syrup:

1 cup canned unsweetened coconut milk

½ cup unsweetened or sweetened shredded coconut, or a combination

½ cup sugar

Sweetened shredded coconut, for garnish

Preheat the oven to 350 degrees. Grease and flour two 9-inch layer pans.

To make the cake: Place the butter and sugar in a mixer fitted with a paddle and mix until light, fluffy, and pale lemon colored, about 3 to 5 minutes. Add the eggs and egg yolks, one at a time, beating well and scraping down the sides of the bowl after each addition.

Place the flour, baking powder, and salt in a mixing bowl and mix to combine.

Scrape down the sides of the bowl, add one-third of the flour mixture, and beat well. Scrape down the sides of the bowl, add ½ cup of the coconut milk, and beat well. Add another third of the flour mixture and beat well. Scrape down the sides of the bowl and add the remaining ½ cup of the coconut milk and the vanilla. Add the remaining third of the flour mixture and beat well. Add the coconut and mix to combine.

Scrape down the sides of the bowl and spoon the batter into the prepared pans. Transfer to the oven and bake until lightly golden and springy on top, about 35 minutes.

To make the syrup: Place the coconut milk, coconut, and sugar in a small saucepan and bring to a boil over medium-high heat. Lower the heat to low and cook until the sugar has melted and the mixture has thickened somewhat, about 4 or 5 minutes.

Cool the cakes in the pans for 5 minutes, invert onto a rack, and split each cake in half horizontally with a serrated knife. Prick holes with a fork and drizzle each warm layer with the warm coconut syrup. Set the cake aside to cool.

While the cake is cooling, make the Seven-Minute Icing, if using. Spread the frosting lightly on each layer. Frost the outside of the cake and sprinkle all over with the coconut. Do not refrigerate.

DESSERT, BUNDT, AND LAYER CAKES

Maxine Weinberg's Black-Bottom Cupcakes

These cupcakes, from my friend Lisa Port White's friend Maxine Weinberg, are a notch above a standard chocolate cupcake: the little cream cheese surprise in each one makes them perfect for children's birthday parties.

For the topping:

6 ounces cream cheese, at room temperature

½ cup sugar

1 egg, at room temperature

½ cup chocolate chips

For the cupcakes:

2¼ cups all-purpose flour

¼ cup plus 2 tablespoons unsweetened cocoa powder

1½ cups sugar

1½ teaspoons baking soda

¾ teaspoon kosher salt

1½ teaspoons white vinegar

1½ teaspoons vanilla extract

½ cup vegetable oil

1½ cups water

Preheat the oven to 350 degrees. Lightly butter or grease 24 muffin tins.

To make the topping: Place all the ingredients in a small bowl, mix well, and set aside.

To make the cupcakes: Place all the ingredients, except the water, in a medium-size mixing bowl and mix until smooth, scraping down the bowl as you mix. Gradually add the water and mix until smooth.

Fill the prepared muffin tins halfway with the batter and top with 1 teaspoon of the topping.

Transfer to the oven and bake until firm, about 20 minutes.

★ YIELD: 24 MUFFINS

DESSERT, BUNDT, AND LAYER CAKES

Mocha Cupcakes

A grown-up cupcake from Bercie's books. Serve alone or with Dark Chocolate Ganache (page 180) or Milk Chocolate Ganache (page 181).

1⅓ cups all-purpose flour

½ cup unsweetened cocoa powder

1 teaspoon baking powder

½ teaspoon baking soda

¼ teaspoon Kosher salt

¼ teaspoon ground cinnamon

1½ teaspoons coffee powder (use espresso powder if you are a coffee fan)

½ cup hot water

1 teaspoon vanilla extract

½ cup whole milk, plain yogurt, or sour cream

¼ pound (1 stick) unsalted butter, at room temperature

1 cup sugar

1 egg

Preheat the oven to 375 degrees. Line 18 muffin cups with paper baking cups.

Place the flour, cocoa powder, baking powder, baking soda, salt, and cinnamon in a bowl and mix to combine.

Place the coffee powder and water in a small bowl and mix until the coffee has dissolved. Add the vanilla and milk and mix until well combined.

Place the butter and sugar in the bowl of a mixer fitted with a paddle and beat until light, fluffy, and light lemon colored, about 3 to 5 minutes. Add the egg and beat well. Scrape down the sides of the bowl, add half of the flour mixture, and beat well. Add the coffee mixture and then the remaining flour mixture.

Scrape down the sides of the bowl and fill the prepared muffin tins two-thirds full. Transfer to the oven and bake until a toothpick inserted in the center comes out clean, about 20 minutes. Set aside to cool.

★ **YIELD: 18 CUPCAKES**

DESSERT, BUNDT, AND LAYER CAKES

Glazes, Ganaches, and Icings

Many of these recipes are interchangeable, unless noted.

TO TRANSPORT GANACHES AND ICINGS

If you are travelling a long distance, you may want to ice your cake at the bake sale. Place the icing in a shallow bowl and cover with aluminum foil or plastic wrap. Remember to bring a knife, a flexible stainless steel spatula, and/or an offset spatula.

Chocolate Glaze

A tiny bit lighter than ganache, this glaze is great when you want a thinner covering. Serve on the Banana Cake (page 151).

4 ounces semisweet chocolate

3 tablespoons heavy cream

3 tablespoons water

½ teaspoon vanilla extract

Place the chocolate in a double boiler over medium heat and cook until almost all the chocolate has melted. Off heat, stir until the chocolate is smooth. Gradually add the cream, water, and vanilla, stirring continuously, until smooth. Set aside to cool.

★ **YIELD: ENOUGH FOR 1 BUNDT OR TWO-LAYER CAKE**

GLAZES,
GANACHES,
AND ICINGS

Dark Chocolate Ganache

Serve on Black Chocolate Cake (page 169), Banana Cake (page 151), and Mocha Cupcakes (page 176).

3 cups semisweet chocolate chips
2 cups heavy cream

Place the chocolate in a double boiler over medium heat and cook until almost all the chocolate has melted. Off heat, stir until the chocolate is smooth. Gradually add the cream, stirring continuously, until smooth. Set aside to cool.

★ YIELD: ENOUGH FOR 1 BUNDT OR TWO-LAYER CAKE

Milk Chocolate Ganache

Serve on the White Chocolate Cake (page 161).

2⅔ cups milk chocolate chips

1 to 1½ cups heavy cream

Place the chocolate in a double boiler over medium heat and cook until almost all the chocolate has melted. Off heat, stir until the chocolate is smooth. Gradually add the cream and stir until smooth. Spread over the cake.

★ **YIELD: ENOUGH FOR 1 BUNDT OR TWO-LAYER CAKE**

GLAZES,
GANACHES,
AND ICINGS

Caramel Icing

Serve on the Banana Cake (page 151) and Black Chocolate Cake (page 169). Be *very* careful when pouring in the cream; the caramel will be very hot and may splatter.

1½ cups sugar

¾ cup heavy cream, at room temperature

Place the sugar in a medium-size saucepan over high heat and cook, stirring frequently, until it starts to caramelize, about 5 to 6 minutes. Lower the heat to medium-low and very, very carefully and gradually add the cream. Stir until completely smooth. Let cool slightly and then pour over the cooled cake.

★ **YIELD: ENOUGH FOR 1 BUNDT OR TWO-LAYER CAKE**

Cream Cheese Icing

Serve on Banana Cake (page 151) and Coconut Cake (page 171).

¼ pound (1 stick) unsalted butter, at room temperature
8 ounces cream cheese, at room temperature (do not use low fat or nonfat)
2 cups confectioners' sugar
2 teaspoons vanilla extract

Place the butter and cream cheese in a mixer fitted with a paddle and beat until smooth. Scrape down the sides of the bowl and carefully and gradually add the sugar and vanilla, continuing to beat.

★ **YIELD: ENOUGH FOR 1 BUNDT OR TWO-LAYER CAKE**

GLAZES,
GANACHES,
AND ICINGS

Seven-Minute Icing

If you don't have a hand-held mixer, this is not the icing to make if you tire easily. Serve on Banana Cake (page 151) and Coconut Cake (page 171).

4 egg whites, at room temperature

1½ cups sugar

⅓ cup water

⅛ teaspoon cream of tartar

1 teaspoon vanilla extract

Pinch kosher salt

Place the egg whites, sugar, water, and cream of tartar in the top of a double boiler over high heat. Beat the mixture with an electric beater, eggbeater, or whisk for 7 minutes. Off heat, add the vanilla and salt and continue beating until the icing holds stiff peaks.

★ YIELD: ENOUGH FOR 1 TWO-LAYER CAKE

Quick Breads, Mini Breads, and Muffins

Although my KitchenAid mixer was supposed to help me make bread from scratch and fill my kitchen with the scent of yeasty dough, more often than not, I use it for making quick breads. They're the perfect breads to make for anyone (like myself) who craves instant gratification.

All these breads can be made into muffins; the equation is one loaf equals 12 to 16 muffins. Simply fill the greased tins halfway, keep your eye on the oven, and decrease the cooking time to 10 to 20 minutes.

TO TRANSPORT AND DISPLAY BREADS

Line a shoe box with a clean dish towel. Place the bread or muffins on a plate, lower to the bottom of the box, and, if necessary, secure by placing toothpicks on the sides of the bread, which will prevent the sides of the bread from touching the sides of the box.

Be sure to cut slices; no one will want to ask you to cut it open. Wrap slices and cupcakes with plastic wrap, if desired.

Cranberry Walnut Bread

I f any quick bread evokes New England, this is it.

½ cup sugar

1¼ cups light brown sugar

Grated zest of 4 oranges

2⅓ cups all-purpose flour

1 tablespoon ground ginger

1 teaspoon ground cinnamon

¼ pound (1 stick) unsalted butter, chilled

2½ teaspoons baking powder

1 teaspoon baking soda

½ teaspoon kosher salt

2 eggs, at room temperature

½ cup sour cream

One 12-ounce bag (about 2½ cups) cranberries

2 cups coarsely chopped toasted walnuts (see note on page 28)

Preheat the oven to 350 degrees. Grease and flour two 9 x 5 x 3-inch pans.

Place the granulated sugar, brown sugar, and orange zest in the bowl of a mixer fitted with a paddle and spin/mix for 5 minutes. Add the flour, ginger, cinnamon, and butter and mix until it resembles sand. Remove ½ cup and set aside.

Add the baking powder, baking soda, and salt and mix well. Add the eggs and sour cream and mix just to combine. Scrape down the sides of the bowl and gently fold in the cranberries and walnuts.

Spoon the batter into the prepared pans. Smooth the tops down and sprinkle with the reserved sugar mixture. Transfer to the oven and bake until a toothpick comes out almost clean, about 45 minutes.

★ **YIELD: 8–10 SLICES PER LOAF**

QUICK BREADS,
MINI BREADS,
AND MUFFINS

Paige's Astounding Banana Bread

There is not one unusual or special ingredient in this banana bread, but it is, hands down, the absolute best. If you're making muffins, bake them for about 15 minutes.

3 or 4 overripe bananas (the nastier the better)
1¼ cups sugar
¼ pound (1 stick) unsalted butter, melted and slightly cooled
2 eggs, at room temperature
1 teaspoon vanilla extract
1½ cups all-purpose flour
½ teaspoon kosher salt
1½ teaspoons baking soda
½ cup chopped toasted walnuts (optional) (see note on page 28)

Preheat the oven to 350 degrees. Lightly grease a 9 x 5 x 3-inch loaf pan.

Place the bananas and sugar in the bowl of a mixer and "whip the bejesus out of them," about 2 or 3 minutes.

Add the butter, eggs, and vanilla, whipping well and scraping down the sides of the bowl before each addition. Scrape down the sides of the bowl, add the flour, salt, baking soda, and nuts, if using, and mix to combine.

Pour into the prepared pan and transfer to the oven. Bake until golden brown and firm in the center, about 1 hour.

★ **YIELD: 12 SLICES, 8 SLABS, OR 16 MUFFINS**

Amy Bodiker's Lemon Poppy Seed Tea Bread

Amy, a former pastry chef who now works at Chefs Collaborative 2000 in Cambridge, Massachusetts, gave me this delightful recipe. She often makes it in small loaf pans to give as gifts.

For the bread:

¾ cup (1½ sticks) unsalted butter, at room temperature

¾ cup sugar

1½ cups all-purpose flour

¾ teaspoon baking powder

½ teaspoon kosher salt

2 tablespoons poppy seeds

3 eggs, at room temperature

¼ cup milk

Zest of 2 lemons

1½ teaspoons vanilla extract

For the soaking syrup:

⅓ cup fresh lemon juice

⅓ cup sugar

Preheat the oven to 350 degrees. Lightly grease one 9 x 3 x 5-inch loaf pan.

Place the butter and sugar in the bowl of a mixer fitted with a paddle and mix until light, fluffy, and pale lemon colored, about 3 to 5 minutes.

Place the flour, baking powder, salt, and poppy seeds in a bowl and toss to combine.

Place the eggs, milk, lemon zest, and vanilla in a bowl and mix well.

Add one-third of the flour mixture and beat well. Scrape down the sides of the bowl and add half the egg mixture, continuing to beat. Repeat with the second third of the flour mixture and the rest of the egg mixture, and then add the remaining one-third dry ingredients, beating after each addition but being careful not to overmix. Scrape down the sides of the bowl and spoon the batter into the pan.

Transfer to the oven and bake until a toothpick comes out clean and the top is just beginning to turn golden, about 45 minutes for the large pans and about 30 to 35 minutes for the smaller pans.

To make the soaking syrup: Place the lemon juice and sugar in a small saucepan and bring to a boil over medium heat. Cook until the sugar is dissolved, stirring continuously.

When the bread comes out of the oven, poke in several places with a skewer and pour half the syrup over the bread. When the bread is cool enough to handle, remove from the pan and brush the bottom and sides with the remaining syrup.

Wrap in plastic wrap and store.

★ **YIELD: 8–10 SLICES**

Helen Fanucci's Applesauce Bread

Helen Fanucci's dad was a minister when she was growing up; contributing to and attending bake sales was almost an everyday occurrence. Although the apple flavor is predominant, the texture of this loaf has more in common with zucchini bread than with apple cake.

When you add the applesauce, the mixture will break. While you may think you've ruined it, just keep going; you haven't. It's just ugly.

2 eggs, at room temperature

¾ to 1 cup sugar

1½ cups applesauce, at room temperature

¼ pound (1 stick) unsalted butter, melted and slightly cooled

1½ cups all-purpose flour

1 teaspoon kosher salt

½ teaspoon ground cinnamon

1½ teaspoons baking soda

1 cup chopped toasted walnuts (see the note on page 28)

Preheat the oven to 350 degrees. Lightly grease a 9 x 3 x 5-inch loaf pan.

Place the eggs and sugar in the bowl of a mixer fitted with a paddle and mix until lemon colored and thickened, about 2 to 3 minutes.

Add the applesauce and butter, beating well and scraping down the sides of the bowl before each addition. Add the flour, salt, cinnamon, baking soda, and nuts and mix to combine.

QUICK BREADS,
MINI BREADS,
AND MUFFINS

Scrape down the sides of the bowl and pour into the prepared pan. Transfer to the oven and bake until golden brown and firm in the center, about 1 hour.

★ YIELD: 8–10 SLICES

THE
BakeSale
Cookbook
★

Fresh Ginger Gingerbread

This is one of the few recipes that I had to rework until it was just right. I was looking for something black and moist. After many, many adjustments I tried blackstrap molasses, which makes all the difference to the taste and appearance.

The optional soaking syrup adds a tartness that I love, but serving it solo is also wonderful.

1½ cups all-purpose flour

½ teaspoon kosher salt

½ teaspoon baking soda

2 teaspoons ground ginger

½ teaspoon ground cinnamon

½ pound (2 sticks) unsalted butter, at room temperature

½ cup brown sugar

1 tablespoon finely minced fresh gingerroot

2 eggs, at room temperature

1 teaspoon vanilla extract

¾ cup blackstrap molasses

½ cup boiling water

For the soaking syrup (optional):

⅓ cup fresh lemon juice

⅓ cup sugar

QUICK BREADS,
MINI BREADS,
AND MUFFINS

Preheat the oven to 350 degrees. Butter a 9-inch pie pan or a 8 x 8-inch pan.

Place the flour, salt, baking soda, ground ginger, and cinnamon in a bowl and mix to combine.

Place the butter, sugar, and fresh gingerroot in the bowl of a mixer fitted with a paddle and beat until light, fluffy, and pale yellow, about 3 to 5 minutes. Add the eggs, one at a time, beating well and scraping down the sides of the bowl before each addition. Add one-third of the flour mixture and beat well. Add the vanilla and ¼ cup of the molasses and beat well. Scrape down the sides of the bowl, add another third of the flour mixture, and beat well. Add the remaining ½ cup molasses and beat well. Add the remaining one-third flour mixture and beat well. Scrape down the sides of the bowl and add the water. Scrape down the sides of the bowl and spoon into the prepared pan.

Transfer to the oven and bake until a tester comes out clean and the top is firm and domed, about 25 to 30 minutes.

To make the soaking syrup: Place the lemon juice and sugar in a pan and bring to a boil over high heat. When the gingerbread comes out of the oven, use a pastry brush to brush the syrup over the top.

★ YIELD: 8–9 PIECES

Green-Flecked Zucchini Bread

When I was in college, my psychology professor Lew Harvey and his wife, Ilse Gayl, invited me to dinner. I had about five recipes in my repertoire and brought this absolutely fabulous zucchini bread, given to me by Susie Fritz, a friend from college. When I told Lew and Ilse what I had brought, they quietly instructed me not to tell Isle's visiting father, who claimed to hate zucchini. He inhaled one piece and then another while the three of us silently chuckled. This bread is so good even zucchini haters will beg for more.

1½ cups sugar

3 eggs, at room temperature

1 cup canola or vegetable oil

2 cups all-purpose flour

2 teaspoons baking soda

¼ teaspoon baking powder

1 teaspoon kosher salt

1 tablespoon ground cinnamon

2 cups grated zucchini

1 cup chopped toasted walnuts or pecans (see note on page 28)

1 tablespoon vanilla extract

Preheat the oven to 350 degrees. Grease two 8 x 4 x 3-inch loaf pans.

Place the sugar, eggs, and oil in the bowl of a mixer fitted with a paddle and beat until thick and lemon colored. Add the flour, baking soda, baking powder, salt, and cinnamon and beat until combined. Scrape down the sides of the bowl, add the zucchini, nuts, and vanilla, and mix until just combined.

Scrape down the sides of the bowl and pour into the prepared pan. Transfer to the oven and bake until a tester comes out clean, about 1 hour. Cool the bread in the pan for 10 minutes and then invert onto a rack. Cool to room temperature.

★YIELD: 8–10 SLICES PER LOAF

THE
BakeSale
Cookbook

Corn Bread

I've been making corn bread often since college, and I still think the best way to eat it is hot out of the oven, slathered with unsalted butter (it must be at room temperature) and honey. Mmmmm.

I have included the option of adding cheese because I know that there are those who love it. However, for my taste, the cheese flavor doesn't come through enough to justify the extra fat and calories.

When the corn bread is no longer moist, cube and toast it for great croutons.

QUICK BREADS,
MINI BREADS,
AND MUFFINS

1¼ cups stone-ground yellow cornmeal

1¼ cups all-purpose flour

2 teaspoons baking powder

1½ teaspoons kosher salt

3 tablespoons honey

¼ cup (4 tablespoons) unsalted butter, melted

1½ cups milk

1 cup creamed corn

2 eggs, at room temperature

1 cup grated salty, hard cheese, such as cheddar or provolone (optional)

Preheat the oven to 375 degrees. Lightly butter an 8 x 8-inch pan.

Place the cornmeal, flour, baking powder, and salt in a medium-size mixing bowl and stir to combine.

Place the honey and butter in the bowl of a mixer fitted with a paddle and beat until light, fluffy, and pale amber colored, about 3 to 5 minutes. Scrape down the sides of the bowl, add the milk, corn, and eggs, and mix well.

Pour the milk mixture and the cheese, if using, into the cornmeal mixture and mix by hand until just combined. Scrape down the sides of the bowl and spoon the mixture into the prepared pan. Transfer to the oven and bake until firm to the touch and light gold on the edges, about 30 minutes.

★ YIELD: ABOUT 16 PIECES

Pumpkin Corn Bread

This gorgeous corn bread is the color of my (controversial) kitchen walls. Though the corn bread is seductive and begs for butter when right out of the oven, it is far more flavorful the next day. If you are not a fan of nutmeg, you can eliminate it.

1¼ cups all-purpose flour

¾ cup stone-ground yellow cornmeal

⅔ cup light brown sugar

1 tablespoon baking powder

½ teaspoon kosher salt

½ teaspoon ground nutmeg

¼ teaspoon ground mace

¾ cup canned pumpkin puree, at room temperature

⅔ cup buttermilk or sour cream

¼ cup (4 tablespoons) unsalted butter, melted

2 eggs, at room temperature and lightly beaten

2 tablespoons honey

1 cup cranberries (optional)

Preheat the oven to 350 degrees. Lightly grease an 8 x 8-inch pan or a 9-inch pie pan.

Place the flour, cornmeal, sugar, baking powder, salt, nutmeg, and mace in a mixing bowl and toss together.

Place the pumpkin puree, buttermilk, butter, eggs, and honey in a mixing bowl and mix until well combined. Add the pumpkin mixture to the flour mixture and mix until just combined. Add the cranberries, if using. Scrape the sides of the bowl and spoon the batter into the prepared pan. Transfer to the oven and bake until the edges just begin to color, about 40 minutes. Cool to room temperature.

★ YIELD: ABOUT 16 PIECES

Pies

My daughter, Lauren, has been swallowing pills since she was two, and when doctors seem surprised, I always say that it's because no one ever told her that it was supposed to be hard. It's the same way with pies: I just never thought they were a big deal, and really, they're not.

I don't mean that I don't love them—I do—but I don't understand why so many pies are so bad. Mine are not always things of beauty (I don't have the patience to make elaborate lattice crusts, for example), but they always taste great. And if you have trouble with the top (which is for me the hardest part), there are two easy outs: use the Crumble Topping (page 207) or roll out the top crust, cut out shapes with a cookie cutter, and overlap the shapes. It's actually even prettier than a whole crust.

TO TRANSPORT AND DISPLAY PIES

Line a box that is at least 2 inches deeper than the pie with a clean dish towel. Lower the pie to the bottom of the box, and, if necessary, secure by surrounding the pie with an additional clean dish towel. My suggestion is to sell only whole pies; just be sure to use aluminum pans.

The recipes in this book make a generous amount for the top and bottom of one 9-inch pie, or top or bottom only for two 9-inch pies. Do not feel that you must use it all; if you can keep your crust thin and end up with lots of scraps, you have done an admirable job. You can use the scraps to make decoration or sprinkle them with cinnamon and sugar and bake them for about 10 minutes on an ungreased cookie sheet for a special treat.

★ Use fresh fruit.

★ Don't overwork the crust.

★ Let the fruit speak for itself. Err on the side of too little sugar and too little thickener.

★ Add the water slowly and use only enough to get the dough to come together.

★ If you have the time, place the ready-to-bake pie in the freezer for 20 to 30 minutes.

★ Start baking on the lowest shelf at 400 to 425 degrees and then decrease the heat to 350 degrees after 10 to 15 minutes.

★ Let pies sit for 10 minutes after you take them out of the oven. Place a perfectly clean dish towel on the pie (to prevent the steam from burning you) and push the top crust down very gently. Remove the towel and then finish cooling.

Butter Piecrust

This is your basic, no-fail pie dough; it can be made in the food processor or by hand.

3 cups all-purpose flour

¾ teaspoon kosher salt

1 to 2 tablespoons sugar

1 teaspoon ground cinnamon

½ pound (2 sticks) unsalted butter, cold or frozen, cut into small bits

4 to 6 tablespoons ice water

Place the flour, salt, sugar, and cinnamon in a food processor and process until combined. Add the butter little by little and process until it has the consistency of coarse cornmeal or is pebbly. Gradually add the water and process until the dough pulls away from the sides. Divide into two disks, cover, and refrigerate until ready to use, at least 1 hour. If you are not going to use it within 1 day, double wrap and freeze it.

Roll out each disk into a 12-inch circle and gently place one in a 9- or 9½-inch pie pan. Place the filling in the pan and place the remaining crust on top of the filling. Flute the edges, if desired. Refrigerate the assembled pie until ready to bake.

Shortening Piecrust

Before making this dough, I had never made a piecrust with solid vegetable shortening. Once I started, this one really intrigued me: it was so easy to work with, had such a great texture when formed into a ball, and lo and behold, it had great flavor when baked. I'm embarrassed to say so, but I guess I'm a reluctant convert.

2¼ cups all-purpose flour
2 tablespoons sugar
¾ teaspoon kosher salt
14 tablespoons solid vegetable shortening
4 to 6 tablespoons ice water

Place the flour, sugar and salt in a food processor fitted with a steel blade and process until combined. Add the shortening and process until the mixture has the consistency of coarse cornmeal or is pebbly. Gradually add the water and process until the dough pulls away from the sides. Divide into two disks, cover, and refrigerate until ready to use, at least 1 hour. If you are not going to use it within 1 day, double wrap and freeze it.

Roll out each disk into a 12-inch circle and gently place one in a 9- or 9½-inch pie pan. Place the filling in the pan and place the remaining crust on top of the filling. Flute the edges, if desired. Refrigerate the assembled pie until ready to bake.

Half-and-Half Dough

3 cups all-purpose flour

1 teaspoon sugar

¾ teaspoon kosher salt

¾ cup (1½ sticks) unsalted butter, cold and cut into pieces

6 tablespoons solid vegetable shortening

4 tablespoons cold water

Place the flour, sugar, and salt in a food processor fitted with a steel blade and process until combined. Add the butter and process until it has been incorporated. Add the shortening and process until the mixture has the consistency of coarse cornmeal or is pebbly. Gradually add the water and process until the dough pulls away from the sides. Divide into two disks, cover, and refrigerate until ready to use, at least 1 hour. If you are not going to use it within 1 day, double wrap and freeze it.

Roll out each disk into a 12-inch circle and gently place one in a 9- or 9½-inch pie pan. Place the filling in the pan and place the remaining crust on top of the filling. Flute the edges, if desired. Refrigerate the assembled pie until ready to bake.

Turnover Dough

Unlike pies, turnovers really should be eaten the day they are made, if not minutes after they come right out of the oven.

Any pie dough (pages 203, 204, and 205)
Any filling
Egg yolk, for brushing
Sugar, for sprinkling

Divide the pie dough into 8 to 10 pieces and form each into a disk. Roll each disk into a 6- or 7-inch circle.

Place about ¼ cup filling on one half of the circle, leaving a border of about ¾ to 1 inch. Place the unfilled part over the filled part and press the edges together. Press the edges with your fingers to seal well and then press again. Cover and refrigerate at least 1 hour.

Preheat the oven to 400 degrees.

Place the turnovers on a baking sheet. Brush with the egg yolk and sprinkle with the sugar. Cut steam vents by making X's or three straight lines with a sharp knife. Transfer to the oven and bake until lightly golden, about 20 to 30 minutes Transfer to a cooling rack and cool to room temperature.

Crumble Topping
for Bottom-Crust-Only Pies

This is a great pie topping for people who love crumbles but want to serve something a little neater.

The crumble should be used right away or chilled for future use. If the mixture gets too soft, the butter will bleed out as soon as it hits the oven. Yuck!

½ cup all-purpose flour

¼ cup light brown sugar

½ teaspoon ground cinnamon

Pinch kosher salt

3 tablespoons unsalted butter, cold

½ cup coarsely chopped toasted walnuts or pecans (see note on page 28)

Preheat the oven to 350 degrees.

Place the flour, sugar, cinnamon, and salt in a large mixing bowl and toss to combine. Add the butter and combine with a pastry cutter or with two forks until it has reached a consistent crumble. Add the nuts. Place on top of the filling and transfer to the oven.

Bake until the top is golden and the fruit is very tender, about 1 hour and 20 minutes, depending upon which pie you are using.

All-American Apple Pie

he name says it all.

For the filling:

7 or 8 Granny Smith apples, peeled, cored, thinly sliced, and chopped

½ cup granulated or light brown sugar, or more to taste (halve if you are using the crumble topping)

1 tablespoon all-purpose flour or 1 ½ to 2 tablespoons cornstarch

1 teaspoon ground cinnamon

1 recipe piecrust (pages 203, 204, 205), your choice

1 recipe Crumble Topping for Bottom-Crust-Only Pies (page 207) (optional)

Preheat the oven to 425 degrees.

Place the apples, sugar, flour, and cinnamon in a bowl and toss well. Place the mixture in the unbaked pie shell and cover with the top crust or Crumble Topping.

Transfer the pie to the lowest shelf in the oven and cook for 15 minutes. Lower the temperature to 350 degrees and cook until the fruit starts to bubble and the crust is golden brown, about 1 hour.

Apple Cranberry Pie

Although this pie makes a great fall dessert, since apples are always available and those with smarts keep a bag of cranberries in the freezer, you can make it year-round.

4 Granny Smith apples, peeled, cored, and thinly sliced

2 cups fresh or frozen cranberries

1 cup sugar

2 tablespoons cornstarch or minute tapioca

1 tablespoon fresh lemon juice

1 recipe piecrust (pages 203, 204, 205), your choice

1 recipe Crumble Topping for Bottom-Crust-Only Pies
(page 207) (optional)

Preheat the oven to 400 degrees.

Place the apples, cranberries, sugar, cornstarch, and lemon juice in a large mixing bowl and toss well. Place the mixture in the unbaked pie shell and cover with the top crust or Crumble Topping.

Transfer the pie to the lowest shelf in the oven and cook for 15 minutes. Lower the heat to 350 degrees and cook until the fruit starts to bubble and the crust is golden brown, about 1 hour.

Peach Blueberry Pie

I f any pie speaks of summer, this is it.

7 or 8 ripe peaches, peeled if desired, quartered, and thinly sliced
1 pint blueberries or blackberries
½ cup sugar
¼ cup all-purpose flour

1 recipe piecrust (pages 203, 204, 205), your choice
1 recipe Crumble Topping for Bottom-Crust-Only Pies
(page 207) (optional)

Preheat the oven to 400 degrees.

Place the peaches, blueberries, sugar, and flour in a large mixing bowl and toss well. Place the mixture in the unbaked pie shell and cover with the top crust or Crumble Topping.

Transfer the pie to the lowest shelf in the oven and cook for 15 minutes. Lower the heat to 350 degrees and cook until the fruit starts to bubble and the crust is golden brown, about 45 to 50 minutes.

Mamama's Peach Pie

"An integral part of this recipe," says Amy Bodiker, "is the Pillsbury crust. Though trained as a baker, I still honor this signature piece of my grandmother's repertoire with this store-bought crust. Serve it warm with vanilla ice cream. It is the perfect end to any summer meal or served cold for breakfast."

One 8-inch Pillsbury ready-made piecrust
4 or 5 ripest, sweetest peaches, pitted, peeled, and halved
1 egg, beaten until smooth
1 cup sugar
2 tablespoons all-purpose flour
1 tablespoon unsalted butter, melted
Dash kosher salt
Dash vanilla extract
Dash almond extract

Preheat the oven to 425 degrees.

Line crust in pie pan, crimping the edges if you're feeling fancy. Fill the pie shell with the peaches, cut side up.

Place the egg, sugar, flour, butter, salt, vanilla, and almond extract in a large mixing bowl and stir until well combined. Pour the mixture over the peaches, filling the holes between the peaches and the depressions left by the stones.

Transfer the pie to the lowest shelf in the oven and bake for 30 minutes. Lower the heat to 350 degrees and bake for an additional 15 minutes. Cool on a wire rack and serve as soon as possible.

Judy Cockerton's Sour Cream–Peach Pie

J udy Cockerton, the owner of No Kidding: A Toy Store, is not the creator of this pie. In fact, I have no knowledge of her ever making it, but the first time I made it she watched me and we talked and talked and talked, and now, whenever I make this pie, I think of Judy.

7 or 8 peaches, pitted, peeled, and sliced or chopped
1 cup sour cream
¼ to ½ cup light brown sugar
1 tablespoon all-purpose flour or cornstarch
1 teaspoon vanilla extract
¼ to ½ teaspoon ground nutmeg
¼ to ½ teaspoon ground cinnamon

1 recipe piecrust (pages 203, 204, 205), your choice
1 recipe Crumble Topping for Bottom-Crust-Only Pies
(page 207) (optional)

Preheat the oven to 400 degrees.

Place the peaches, sour cream, sugar, flour, vanilla, nutmeg, and cinnamon in a bowl and toss well. Place the mixture in the un-baked pie shell and cover with the top crust or Crumble Topping.

Transfer the pie to the lowest shelf in the oven and cook for 15 minutes. Lower the heat to 350 degrees and cook until the fruit starts to bubble and the crust is golden brown, about an additional 1 hour and 15 to 20 minutes. Cool to room temperature.

Mark's Favorite: Fresh Blueberry Pie

My husband, Mark, loves blueberry pie and swears that a certain restaurant in Westport, Massachusetts, has the best blueberry pie ever. No way, I say.

2½ to 3 pints fresh blueberries

⅔ to ¾ cup sugar

¼ cup all-purpose flour or 3 tablespoons cornstarch

½ to 1 teaspoon finely grated lemon zest (optional)

1 recipe Butter Piecrust (page 203)

Preheat the oven to 400 degrees.

Place the blueberries, sugar, flour, and lemon zest, if using, in a large mixing bowl and toss well. Place the mixture in the unbaked pie shell and cover with the top crust.

Transfer the pie to the lowest shelf in the oven and cook for 15 minutes. Lower the heat to 350 degrees and cook until the fruit starts to bubble and the crust is golden brown, about an additional 30 to 45 minutes. Cool to room temperature.

Strawberry Rhubarb Pie

Mark's uncle Tom Linane gave us a rhubarb plant several years ago. Since it is a productive little plant, I can now make my favorite desserts: strawberry rhubarb compote, crumble, or pie—at a moment's notice. I have also discovered that thinly sliced rhubarb takes kindly to freezing.

This pie is almost always a bit runny, which is fine with me, but if you want a firmer pie, add another tablespoon of cornstarch. It won't taste quite as good, but it will be neater.

You can substitute an equal amount of blueberries for the strawberries.

3 cups thinly sliced rhubarb
1 quart strawberries, quartered or sliced
½ to ¾ cup sugar
3 tablespoons cornstarch

1 recipe piecrust (pages 203, 204, 205), your choice

Preheat the oven to 400 degrees.

Place the rhubarb, strawberries, sugar, and cornstarch in a bowl and toss well. Place the mixture in the unbaked pie shell and cover with the top crust.

Transfer the pie to the lowest shelf in the oven and cook for 15 minutes. Lower the heat to 350 degrees and cook until the fruit starts to bubble and the crust is golden brown, about an additional 45 minutes to 1 hour.

Ginger Pear Pie

P ears and ginger are a combination made in heaven.

7 to 8 ripe pears, quartered and thinly sliced

½ to ¾ cup sugar

3 to 4 tablespoons all-purpose flour

2 teaspoons finely chopped fresh gingerroot

1 recipe piecrust (pages 203, 204, 205), your choice

1 recipe Crumble Topping for Bottom-Crust-Only Pies

(page 207) (optional)

Preheat the oven to 400 degrees.

Place the pears, sugar, flour, and gingerroot in a bowl and toss well. Place the mixture in the unbaked pie shell and cover with the top crust or Crumble Topping.

Transfer the pie to the oven and cook for 15 minutes. Lower the heat to 350 degrees and cook until the fruit starts to bubble and the crust is golden brown, about an additional 45 minutes.

Variation:

FOR GINGER FIG PIE, ADD:

½ CUP CHOPPED DRIED FIGS OR 8 QUARTERED FRESH FIGS

2 TO 3 TABLESPOONS ARMAGNAC

TO THE FILLING INGREDIENTS.

Gran Otto's Dirty Pie

Our friends Meghan Floyd and Tony Arauz came from Kentucky to spend last summer with us. When I served Mark's Favorite: Fresh Blueberry Pie (page 213), a surprising first for both of them, the talk turned to pies. They bragged about Tony's grandmother's chocolate nut pie, and he volunteered her recipe. Mary Lee (aka Gran Otto) sent her recipe, which received raves from my testers: my five-year-old Ben called it Dirty Pie.

1 recipe piecrust (pages 203, 204, 205), your choice

¼ cup unsalted butter or margarine, at room temperature

1 cup sugar

3 eggs, beaten

½ cup semisweet chocolate chips

½ cup light corn syrup

1 teaspoon vanilla extract

¼ teaspoon salt

½ to 1 cup chopped pecans, toasted if desired (see note on page 28)

1½ tablespoons bourbon

Preheat the oven to 375 degrees.

Place the butter, sugar, and eggs in a bowl and mix to combine. Add the remaining ingredients and mix well. Pour into the un-baked pie shell and transfer to the oven. Bake until just set, about 40 minutes. Set aside to cool to room temperature.

Beverages

Bake sales often offer coffee, but I think it's nice to have a few options for kids.

Lemonade Three Ways

I'll confess that I don't turn up my nose at frozen, but this is so, so much better.

2 cups sugar

4 cups boiling water

12 cups cold water

Juice of 24 lemons (about 6 to 7 cups)

8 lemons, thinly sliced

Fresh-brewed iced tea (optional)

Cranberry juice or Kool-Aid ice cubes (optional)

First way: Place the sugar and boiling water in a heatproof glass and stir until the sugar has dissolved. Set aside to cool to room temperature, then cover and refrigerate for at least 1 hour and up to overnight. Transfer to a pitcher, add the remaining ingredients, and serve in ice-filled glasses.

Second way: Mix half iced tea and half lemonade.

Third way: Use cranberry juice or Kool-Aid ice cubes.

★ **YIELD: ABOUT 24 CUPS**

Sharon Smith's Fruit Punch

Sharon combines these juices for a refreshingly sweet, tart, and sour drink. She prefers using Adam and Eve brand cranberry juice (which has no added sugar), if available.

8 cups cranberry juice

8 cups grapefruit juice

8 cups orange juice

Place all the juices in a large container and stir to combine. Pour into pitchers and serve within 2 to 3 days.

★ YIELD: ABOUT 24 CUPS

BEVERAGES

Index

INDEX

METRIC EQUIVALENCIES

★ Liquid and Dry Measure Equivalencies ★

CUSTOMARY	METRIC
¼ teaspoon	1.25 milliliters
½ teaspoon	2.5 milliliters
1 teaspoon	5 milliliters
1 tablespoon	15 milliliters
1 fluid ounce	30 milliliters
¼ cup	60 milliliters
⅓ cup	80 milliliters
½ cup	120 milliliters
1 cup	240 milliliters
1 pint (2 cups)	480 milliliters
1 quart (4 cups; 32 ounces)	960 milliliters (.96 liter)
1 gallon (4 quarts)	3.84 liters
1 ounce (by weight)	28 grams
¼ pound (4 ounces)	114 grams
1 pound (16 ounces)	454 grams
2.2 pounds	1 kilogram (1,000 grams)

★ Oven Temperature Equivalents ★

DESCRIPTION	°FAHRENHEIT	°CELSIUS
Cool	200	90
Very slow	250	120
Slow	300–325	150–160
Moderately slow	325–350	160–180
Moderate	350–375	180–190
Moderately hot	375–400	190–200
Hot	400–450	200–230
Very hot	450–500	230–260